Philosophers in Perspective

There is an abundance now of books of 'readings' from
the major philosophers, in which the selections are so
often too brief and snippety to be of any great value to
the student. There are also many collections of essays
and articles about the major philosophers on the mar-
ket. These too are unsatisfactory from the student's
point of view in that they suffer severely from the defect of discontinuity and are unable to trace the scope
and articulation of a man's work, as each contributor
writes from the standpoint of his own interpretation.

There is a great need for books that are devoted to a
single philosopher and that are written by a single
author who is allowed the room to develop both his
exposition and his examination of his subject in sufficient detail. *Philosophers in Perspective* satisfies this
demand and makes available to students studies of all
the major philosophers, and some of the undeservedly
minor ones as well, which will afford them for the first
time the opportunity of understanding the philosopher,
of coming to grips with his thought, and of seeing him
in his place in the development of philosophy, or of
his special area of it.

Each book in the series fits into this framework, but
the authors are given the freedom to adapt it to their
own requirements. Main emphasis will be placed on
exposition and examination of the philosopher's
thought, but enough will be written about the influences on him and about his own influence on subsequent thought, to show where he stands in the
perspective of his subject. Wherever relevant, particular emphasis will be placed on the philosopher's
contributions to moral and political thought, which
have often in the past been treated cursorily as tail-
pieces to his writings on metaphysics and epistemology.
This aspect . . . . ve most useful to
students o . . .

Ac

D1143887

Philosophers in Perspective

General Editor: A. D. Woozley

Published titles
Kant: The Philosophy of Right: Jeffrie G. Murphy
John Stuart Mill: A Critical Study: H. J. McCloskey

Forthcoming titles
Aristotle: J. L. Ackrill
Hegel: H. B. Acton
Berkeley: H. M. Bracken
The French Enlightenment: J. H. Brumfitt
Wittgenstein: Cora Diamond
Descartes: Alan Gewirth
Jean-Jacques Rousseau: J. C. Hall
Karl Marx: Eugene Kamenka
Hobbes: J. Kemp
Spinoza: Douglas Lewis
Jeremy Bentham: David Lyons
John Locke: J. D. Mabbott
David Hume: T. Penelhum
Plato: Colin Strang

JOHN STUART MILL:
A CRITICAL STUDY

H. J. McCloskey

Macmillan
St Martin's Press

First published 1971 by
MACMILLAN AND CO LTD
London and Basingstoke
Associated companies in New York Toronto
Dublin Melbourne Johannesburg and Madras

Library of Congress catalog card no. 78–124952

✓SBN 333 08954 5 (hard cover)

Printed in Great Britain by
RICHARD CLAY (THE CHAUCER PRESS), LTD
Bungay, Suffolk

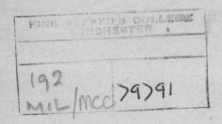

Contents

1 Mill's Life

Mill is among the great figures of the Western world. He exercised a considerable influence in his own day, and his influence seems certain to continue long beyond the present time. Yet, although he made important, lasting contributions to philosophy, Mill is not among the greatest philosophers of the Western world, and even within the British Empiricists, Hume, Locke and Berkeley rank ahead of him. As a philosopher he was unusual in the immediate recognition his work received, in being a man of parts, an economist whose work, while lacking any great claim to originality, was an immediate popular success, a publicist, a leader of thought, a power in the sphere of politics, albeit only briefly a Member of Parliament, and an administrator when he became Chief Examiner in the East India Company. Mill was educated to be a utilitarian and political radical, but because he was ready to examine and attend to the views of all but a few contemporary opponents, his writings are important as meeting places of much of the thought of his times. His life is of especial interest because of the extraordinary education to which his father subjected him (one cannot but wonder whether he might not have been a greater philosopher and public figure had he been more fortunate in his early education), because of his deep, strange, almost unique, rewarding yet frustrating lover –friend relationship with the beautiful, intelligent Harriet Taylor, and because of his impact on his age, and on the world at large. Mill was known to and knew, was influenced by and influenced, many of the great figures of his day, the most notable exception being Karl Marx, of whom Mill appears to have had no knowledge, and who paid his tribute to Mill in *Capital* in the comparative gentleness of his comment on him. (Vol. I, Pt VII, xxiv, 5.) The *Autobiography* is of interest both in itself and for what it omits and inaccurately reports, and consequently needs to be read in conjunction with other sources such as the letters, diaries and comments of his contemporaries, especially Bain and Carlyle.

James Mill

John Stuart Mill was born in London on 20 May 1806, the first son of James and Harriet Mill. James Mill, who himself later became a noted although minor philosopher, was a Scot who, after abandoning a career in the ministry, had come to London. He achieved success and ultimately fame, first through making Benthamism the effective political force it became, especially but not only through the Radicals, as he had the skill to present Bentham's thought and to organise and make effective those in sympathy with it; secondly through his writings, the *Essay on Government, History of India, Elements of Political Economy* and *The Analysis of the Phenomena of the Human Mind*; thirdly as Chief Examiner in the East India Company; and fourthly through his son, John Stuart, who for some years was not unkindly referred to as 'a manufactured man'.

Education

John was taught by his father. He learnt Greek and arithmetic between the ages of three and eight, commencing geometry and algebra towards the end of this period, and reading some Platonic dialogues at the age of seven. At eight he commenced Latin, and between the ages of eight and twelve read Plato's more important dialogues, Homer, Virgil, Horace, Livy, Sallust and Ovid. At eleven he helped his father in the correction of the proofs of the *History of India*. The next year he commenced studying logic, and the following

8

year political economy. For leisure he read mainly histories, *Don Quixote, Robinson Crusoe* and *Arabian Nights.* At seven he taught his sister, Wilhelmina, and thereafter had the responsibility of teaching his brothers and sisters, a task he greatly disliked. During this period Mill saw much of his father's friends, Bentham, Ricardo, Grote, Place and Austin, the Mills living next door to Bentham from 1814 to 1830 in London, and spending a number of summers with him at Ford Abbey in Somerset. At fourteen, John visited France for a year as guest of Sir Samuel Bentham, brother of Jeremy, continuing his education on a broader horizon, in chemistry, zoology, botany, fencing and dancing. On his return to London he resumed his studies under his father's supervision, and again became his brothers' and sisters' teacher. At sixteen he read law with John Austin. His general reading extended widely into philosophy, particularly into Benthamite literature including Dumont's edition of Bentham's *Traité de Législation.* Although his mother and sisters attended church, he was brought up without any religion. He had no friends of his own age. Towards his father he felt respect and fear, not love, his father being sarcastic, bad-tempered and given to making unreasonable demands. John shared his father's lack of respect for his mother.

East India Company

When Mill was seventeen, his father decided his career by having him appointed his subordinate in the East India Company. This choice disappointed Mill, who had hoped for a public career. Professor Townshend tried to get John entered for Cambridge. Sir John Stuart had left money for this purpose, and Grote and Ricardo, but apparently not John himself, remonstrated with his father. James had a religious objection to the universities, and also wished John to have a secure income so that he could provide for his, James's, children should this become necessary. Mill remained at the East India Company until its dissolution in 1858, became Chief Examiner and prepared the case against its dissolution. He seems never to have found any conflict or tension between this work and his espousal of liberalism. He never visited India, nor did he ever seem to deem such a visit important and desirable. His hours of work were 10 a.m. to 4 p.m., his work taking on average three hours a day; hence it was that he was able to see many of his friends and to write much of his philosophy during working hours. At work and elsewhere he always wore black.

Activities up to the First Crisis

During the years 1822 to 1826 Mill led a very active life. His first publication was in the *Traveller* in 1822; it was followed by articles in the *Westminster Review* (founded by Bentham with Bowring as editor in 1823–4). He edited Bentham's *Rationale of Judicial Evidence* at the age of nineteen; for three years, until 1826, he met with friends in the Utilitarian Society at Bentham's house. With many others, including Roebuck, Thirlwall, the Villiers brothers, Romilly, Charles Austin, Macaulay, Henry Taylor, Samuel Wilberforce, Bulwer-Lytton and Fonblanque among others, he helped the economist McCulloch to get the Debating Society established. Through this society he was to come to know d'Eichthal, Sterling and Maurice. During this period he learnt German from Sarah Austin (his *Mütterlein*), the wife of John Austin. He was involved in a brush with his father over his friendship with Roebuck and asserted his independence, but Roebuck never again visited his home.

Crises and Health

In 1826 Mill experienced a period of melancholy which he dramatically described in the *Autobiography* as 'A crisis in my mental history'. He suffered a loss of faith and life seemed to have no meaning. The turning point was the reading of the description of the father's death in Marmontel's *Mémoires*. At this time he turned to poetry, reading Wordsworth for the first time in 1828. This was the period of his reaction against his father and Benthamism. A more serious crisis, not mentioned in the *Autobiography*, occurred at the end of 1835 and into 1836 when his father was dying, Mill withdrawing from the Debating Society. This crisis left him with a permanent tic over one eye. He took three months' sick leave. His father died of tuberculosis that year. For the next twenty years Mill's life was punctuated by periods of ill-health and sick leave; 1839 (six months' sick leave), 1848 (injury to hip, the treatment thereof leading to impaired vision for nearly a year), 1854 (tuberculosis was diagnosed: eight months' sick leave on tour abroad, in Italy and Greece). His brother Henry died of tuberculosis in 1840, George died of the same family disease in 1853, and Harriet was to die of it, probably having contracted it from John, in 1858. From 1854 Mill's work seems rarely to have been interrupted by ill-health. None the less his productivity is remarkable in view of his periods of ill-health.

Harriet Taylor

In 1830 Mill met John and Harriet Taylor at the home of William Fox, Harriet then being twenty-two and the mother of two children. Taylor was a Unitarian, of enlightened, liberal principles, active in helping political refugees, on the committee for the establishment of London University and in business as a wholesale druggist. Until the meeting with Mill, the marriage was a happy one. Mill and Harriet appear to have responded to one another immediately, and although in the *Autobiography* Mill reported that it was some years before the relationship became an intimate one, the earliest relevant letter (probable date August 1832) suggests the contrary, beginning as it does: 'Bénie soit la main qui a tracé ces caractères!

Elle m'a écrit – il suffit.' Mill's affair with Harriet, because of its lack of fulfilment, did not become one of the great love affairs of history; instead, while having marks of such, it hovered between the tragic and the ridiculous. Mill was infatuated with Harriet until her death, and would gladly have married her, had she chosen to obtain a divorce. They travelled together on the Continent, and in England Mill dined each week at Harriet's home, while Taylor dined at his club. The affair not surprisingly provoked gossip and scandal, and caused great hurt to Taylor. It earned Mill reproaches from his father and friends, and advice from others, Mill usually falling out with those inclined to be critical. Most biographers accept Mill's assurance that he and Harriet were not adulterers, Ruth Borchardt plausibly arguing that Harriet found sexuality disgusting, while Bain observed that 'in the so-called sensual feelings, he [Mill] was below average.... He made light of the difficulty of controlling the sexual appetite.' Much has been written about this relationship, most interest centring on Harriet's ability and influence. Mill's tributes to Harriet are so obviously extravagant that, as Bain observed, 'he outraged all reasonable credibility in describing her matchless genius, without being able to supply any corroborating testimony'. Harriet's writings provide no grounds for supposing her to have been a genius or even a person of outstanding gifts, yet it is clear that she was a person of high intelligence. She had a considerable influence on Mill, both because they shared many of the same views, and because of his weakness of character which led him to exaggerate his agreement and to understate the extent of his disagreement with others with whom he was friendly. Harriet, in consistency with his own views, checked him when he understated his disagreement with Comte and flirted with seriously illiberal features of Comte's theories; and because of her greater sympathy with socialism, she led Mill to consider its claims more carefully and to make, at her instigation, appropriate changes to the 2nd and 3rd editions of the *Political Economy*. Taylor died in 1849. Mill and Harriet married in 1851. Their relationship had been a guilt-ridden one, about which they were hypersensitive. When they married, Mill was quick to see slights and discourtesies, especially from his mother, sisters and brother George. He behaved callously and disgracefully towards both George and his mother when they were dying. The absence of any reference to his mother in the *Autobiography* is probably due to this break with his family. Before his death there was a reconciliation with his sister Mary whose children he helped. Before their marriage they had withdrawn from society; after it they were near-recluses in their home at Blackheath. Harriet died at Avignon in 1858. Mill bought a cottage overlooking the cemetery in which she was buried, reportedly furnishing it in part with furniture from the room in which she died. One of the most remarkable features of their relationship was his very great dependence on her; he needed her guidance even in dealing with his neighbour and the rat-catcher.

Friends and Influences

Even before he produced his first major work, the *System of Logic* (completed in 1841, rejected by Murray and published by Parker in 1843), Mill had written very many articles of a wide-ranging character, relating to philosophy, economics, politics, French affairs (he became the best-informed writer on this subject), literature, poetry (he was the first notable figure to recognise Tennyson's poetry) and botany, revealing the leading influences on him, in addition to those of Bentham and James Mill, and at the same time attracting other influences towards him. This rate of productivity continued until his death, but the writings in the period up to and including the *Political Economy* reveal the major influences. He was influenced by Colcridge and the English–German school, and through them by Goethe but not by Hegel. Sterling became, next to Harriet, his closest life's friend. His *The Spirit*

of the Age, influenced by Saint-Simonianism and by
Comte, attracted Carlyle's attention, Carlyle seeing its
author as 'a new mystic', and it led to what for a time
was a valuable friendship for both. He was influenced
by Saint-Simon through d'Eichthal; he corresponded
with Comte, for a time being much impressed by
Comte's theories, and influenced towards seriously
illiberal positions, before, with the help of Harriet, ex-
tricating himself from his unintended discipleship; he
also arranged financial help for a not very grateful
Comte. Mill was quick to appreciate the worth of de
Tocqueville's writings on democracy in America, and
his comments were appreciated as accurate by de Tocqueville. Mill edited the *London Review* (later to become the *London and Westminster Review*) from 1834
to 1837, buying it in the latter year, and later dispos-
ing of it to Hickson, incurring a substantial loss.
Through his association with the *Review* Mill was able
to help unrecognised talent, particularly as he did not
seek to make it a strict, party review. He accepted the
opportunity it gave him to help Carlyle, especially but
not only by his very favourable review of the history of
the French Revolution (he and Harriet had carelessly
mishandled the manuscript of the first volume, which
was destroyed while in their care, Carlyle having no
drafts from which to work); he also effectively supported Durham's handling of affairs in Canada. He was
vocal on Irish matters during 1846–7.

After his wife's death and his retirement on a
generous pension on the dissolution of the East India
Company in 1858, Helen Taylor, his stepdaughter,
became his devoted companion, housekeeper and
secretary. They lived much of the year at Avignon, the
remainder at Blackheath. During this period *On
Liberty* (1859, but written some years earlier), *Utilitarianism* (first published in *Fraser's Magazine*, 1861),
Representative Government (1861), *An Examination
of Sir William Hamilton's Philosophy* (1865), *Auguste
Comte and Positivism* (1865), *The Subjection of
Women* (1869), together with many essays, were published, and parts of the *Autobiography*, *Theism*, and

14

the chapters on socialism (published posthumously) were written, and his father's *Analysis of the Phenomena of the Human Mind* edited. In 1865 he was elected to the House of Commons after the briefest of campaigns, conducted without his financial support. At a working-men's meeting Mill and the workers distinguished themselves, he by acknowledging that he had charged the working men of England with being 'generally liars', and they by applauding his acknowledgement. His most notable success in Parliament was in rallying an unexpectedly strong minority vote for women's franchise. He was defeated in 1868 at least in part because of his contribution to Bradlaugh's election fund. During this period he had a wide range of friends and acquaintances, his close friends including Grote, Bain, Thornton and John Morley, his dinner parties at Blackheath being attended by these and the Amberleys (he became Bertrand Russell's godfather), Fawcett, Cairnes, Herbert Spencer and others. His correspondence as a world figure was immense. He died of a local fever at Avignon in May 1873. Shortly before his death he murmured to Helen, 'You know I have done my work.'

Mill's contributions to logic are spread over many writings, from his review of Whately's *Elements of Logic* (1827), *A System of Logic* (1843; 8th ed., 1872), *An Examination of Sir William Hamilton's Philosophy* (1865), especially chaps 15 to 23, and including the *Inaugural Address at the University of St Andrews* (1867). Mill explained logic as 'the entire theory of the ascertainment of reasoned or inferred truth' (*Logic*, II, 3, 8). He regarded formal, deductive, syllogistic logic (logic of consistency) as of lesser importance, as not relating to real inference; hence his more important contributions concern *language* (names, meaning, definition, ideal language) and *induction* (causality and inductive methods of discovery and proof of causal generalisations). Although the *Logic* is still an important, relevant work today, the contributions of various of Mill's contemporaries and near-contemporaries, for example Boole, de Morgan and Frege, have influenced and have greater relevance to contemporary logical inquiries, while in induction there is an increasing awareness of the writings of Whewell, Jevons and other nineteenth-century inductive logicians, and hence a more accurate placing of Mill's contributions.

Names, Meaning and Definition

Mill explained meaning by reference to connotation and denotation thus:

A non-connotative term is one which signifies a subject only, or an attribute only. A connotative term is one which denotes a subject, and implies an attribute. By a subject is here meant anything which possesses attributes. Thus John, or London, or England, are names which signify a subject only. Whiteness, length, virtue, signify an attribute only. None of these names, therefore, are connotative. But *white, long, virtuous* are connotative. The word white, denotes all white things, as snow, paper, the foam of the sea, etc., and implies, or in the language of the schoolmen, *connotes*, the attribute of *whiteness*. The word white is not predicated of the attribute, but of the subjects, snow, etc.; but when we predicate it of them, we convey the meaning that the attribute whiteness belongs to them.... All concrete general names are connotative.... The name [man], therefore, is said to signify the subjects *directly*, the attributes *indirectly*; it *denotes* the subjects, and implies, or involves, or indicates, or as we shall say henceforth *connotes* the attributes. It is a connotative name.... Proper names are not connotative: they denote the individuals who are called by them; but they do not indicate or imply any attributes as belonging to those individuals.... Proper names are attached to objects themselves, and are not dependent on the continuance of any attribute of the object. (*Logic*, 1, 2, 5)

Thus Mill's considered view was that the connotation of a name was its meaning, and that with connotative names, connotation determined denotation. Mill explained the meaning of non-connotative names, i.e. proper and abstract names, in terms of their denotations, the definition of a non-connotative name being said to be its denotation. With connotative names the statement of the connotation was said to be the definition, Mill observing that 'to fix the connotation of a concrete name, or the denotation of the corresponding abstract, is to define the name' (*Logic*, iv, 4, 3). Such an account seems clear and unequivocal; in fact Mill sometimes wrote as if a definition is a contingent statement, as this suggests, that what is meant by one name is what is meant by other names, a definition of brother being of the form 'What is meant by brother is what is meant by male sibling.' At other times he wrote that the definition provides an analysis of the whole referred to in the subject, the definition analysing it into its component attributes. The former view is suggested by the first, and the latter by the second of the following statements:

> In distinguishing, however, the different kinds of matters of fact asserted in propositions, we reserved one class of propositions, which do not relate to any matter of fact, in the proper sense of the term, at all, but to the meaning of names. Since names and their signification are entirely arbitrary, such propositions are not strictly speaking, susceptible of truth or falsity, but only of conformity or disconformity to usage or convention; and all the proof they are capable of, is proof of usage; proof that words have been employed by others in the acceptation in which the speaker or writer desires to use them. (*Logic*, 1, 6, 1)

> It is, therefore, not without reason that Condillac and other writers have affirmed a definition to be an *analysis*. To resolve any complex whole into the elements of which it is compounded, is the meaning of analysis; and this we do when we replace one word which connotes a set of attributes collectively, by two or more which connote the same attributes singly, or in smaller groups. (*Logic*, 1, 8, 1)

The most important of the many difficulties in the way of the former account is that the gap between language and the world definitions are supposedly used to bridge, would not be bridged by them, and ostensive definitions would be required to perform this role. Yet the account of definitions as analyses would seem to involve Mill in one or other of the theories of universals, conceptualist or realist, which he explicitly rejected. Other accounts are suggested in Mill's treatment of definitions in mathematics, e.g. that they are empirical statements, true in the case of arithmetic,

18

false in geometry. However, Mill's considered view was that the definition set out the attributes referred to in the subject, i.e. that they were analytic propositions, true by definition, and in this *sense* merely verbal and not real propositions. He therefore rejected the Aristotelian theory of real definitions, of things *per genus et differentiam*. The Aristotelian theory of the Predicables – Definition (*genus* et *differentiam*), *proprium, accidens* – turned on the belief that things fell into natural kinds, that language is geared to these kinds, and that real definitions are of things in the sense of defining natural kinds by reference to their essential properties *qua* the kind concerned. Mill did not deny that there were natural kinds, although he explained them otherwise than did Aristotle and the Scholastics; for him the concept of a class was more basic and relevant:

> A general name is familiarly defined, a name which is capable of being truly affirmed in the same sense, of each of an indefinite number of things. ... It is not unusual, by way of explaining what is meant by a general name, to say that it is the name of *a class*. But this, though a convenient mode of expression for some purposes, is objectionable as a definition, since it explains the clearer of the two things by the more obscure. It would be more logical to reverse the proposition, and turn it into a definition of the word *class*: 'A class is the indefinite multitude of individuals denoted by a general name'. (*Logic*, I, 2, 3)

> By a Kind, ... we mean one of those classes which are distinguished from all others not by one or few definite properties, but by an unknown multitude of them; the combination of properties on which the class is grounded being a mere index to an indefinite number of other distinctive attributes. (*Logic*, IV, 6, 4)

Mill was thus obviously indebted to Locke's thesis that 'Nature makes the similitude, Men determine the

19

sorts', even though he rejected much of Locke's treatment of real and nominal essences, including his account of abstract ideas. As against the Aristotelian theory, he argued that definitions are merely verbal, not real propositions, that they convey simply the meanings of names, not information about the world, that so-called essential propositions are merely verbal, either giving no information, or giving it respecting the name, not the thing. Mill's awareness that his account involved him in a problem of explaining the importance of these merely verbal propositions appears to have influenced him in respect of 'definitions' in arithmetic to deny that they are really definitions, and to argue that they are real propositions, being either categorical or hypothetical empirical generalisations. With definitions of non-mathematical kinds, he suggested that they remind us that one thing is a mark of another thing. This, however, hardly suffices as an explanation. Further, if what is claimed to be true of non-mathematical definitions is really true, it ought also to be taken to hold of mathematical definitions unless good reasons to the contrary are offered.

Mill had a clearer grasp of the complexity of language than many of his contemporaries. He acknowledged Dugald Stewart's discussion (which was indebted to Payne Knight) of what is an anticipation of Wittgenstein's account of family names, Mill noting that not all apparent general names are such, that words may come to be applied to things with nothing in common, or to things, each of which has something in common with another member of the collection. In Book I he noted that 'names creep on from subject to subject, until all traces of a common meaning sometimes disappear', and in Book IV he accepted Stewart's point that a name may be applied first to A, then to B which has something in common with A, then to C which has something in common with B but not with A, and so on. (See Dugald Stewart's *Philosophical Essays*, 4th ed., p. 217.) Wittgenstein later restated this point by reference to the word 'game', coining the expression 'family name' to refer to such words. (See

Philosophical Investigations, paras. 66–7.) Awareness of these facts and that not all general names have clear connotations led Mill to suggest that ordinary language is not an ideal philosophical language, that each name should have a clear and distinct connotation. While he noted that language was a dynamic thing and, in agreement with the Coleridge school, that it is a repository of ideas of other ages, he did not fully appreciate the importance of growth and the impossibility of rendering language static in meaning and yet retaining its utility as a means of communication. Were things sharply cut off in the world, and the world not subject to change, the idea of such an ideal language would be more relevant. Ordinary language can express, or expresses more simply and elegantly than an 'ideal' language, many facts because it possesses open-textured words such as 'vehicle', vague words such as 'bald', family words such as 'game', words such as 'life' which admit of use by analogy of proportionality, and also because it admits of figurative uses of ordinary words; it may even allow us to express what a more 'perfect' language may render inexpressible. Compare here poetry and prose. Formal systems (ideal languages of a different sort perhaps) are used to achieve part of what Mill hoped to achieve by revising ordinary language.

General Names and Universals

Mill repudiated the view that general names refer to real universals such as Platonic forms, and was very critical of Locke's account in terms of abstract ideas, and instead explained them as names of attributes defining a class. Yet although he often wrote as if he accepted a nominalist view (e.g. *Hamilton,* 5th ed., chap. 17, p. 387), he did not accept an extreme nominalist view that all that is common to things called by the one general name is the name. He defined general names by reference to classes, and a class in terms of its members possessing a common attribute or

21

attributes. He argued that an attribute such as whiteness is simply the instances of whiteness and, on this basis supposed that there is no real problem concerning universals. But there is a problem, one which cannot be dismissed by a curt insistence that attributes exist only in the objects which instantiate them; consider the significance of talk about attributes which are never instantiated. Mill's treatment of mathematics is relevant here, various critics plausibly arguing that at times he moved towards a realist view in this context. In fact his most usual implicit view, and that most consistent with his phenomenalism, is a conceptualist one, but a conceptualism which involves no reference to abstract ideas.

Deduction and the Syllogism

Traditionally deductive inference had been explained in terms of immediate and mediate inferences, where all mediate inference was in turn explained in terms of the categorical syllogism. Mill argued that since in immediate inference one ends with the same proposition as that with which one begins, there is no advance in knowledge, and no real inference (*Logic*, II, 1). With mediate inference, following Whately and the traditionalists, Mill accepted the view that all valid forms of ratiocination could be reduced to syllogistic form, that 'all correct ratiocination admits of being stated in syllogisms of the first figure alone' (*Logic*, II, 2, 2). The value of traditional attempts to reduce all deductive forms of argument to the one syllogistic form would be widely questioned today. There are many distinct types of arguments, and clarity of thought and the checking of the validity of such arguments are usually not aided by attempts to display them as being of syllogistic form. Consider here the following: most B's are A's, most B's are C's, therefore some A's are C's; if A is B, C is D, A is B, therefore C is D; A is to the left of B, B is to the left of C, therefore A is to the left of C; either A is B or C is D, A is B, therefore C is not D;

$2 + 2 = 4$; only one person failed in Logic last year, namely John Smith. Jill Jones was a candidate and must therefore have passed.

The Syllogism: Its Principle

Aristotle had explained the principle of 'the perfect figure' of the syllogism as that which is now known as *the dictum de omni et nullo*: 'When one thing is predicated of another, all that is predicable of the predicate will be predicable also of the subject' (*Categories*, 1a, 10). 'That one term should be included in another as in a whole is the same as for the other to be predicated of all the first. And we say that one term is predicated of all of another, whenever no instance of the subject can be found of which the other term cannot be asserted: "to be predicated of none" must be understood in the same way' (*Prior Analytics*, 24b, 25, W. D. Ross translation). As R. M. Eaton noted, these statements admit of being interpreted either extensionally, as about classes, or intensionally, as concerning concepts or universals, and were sometimes interpreted the one way and sometimes the other by Aristotle. (See *General Logic*, pt II, chap. ii.) Mill, having rejected real universals, in terms of his theory of classes interpreted the *dictum* as an analytic principle about classes thus: 'Whatever can be affirmed (or denied) of a class, may be affirmed (or denied) of everything included in the class' (*Logic*, II, 2, 2). Although in the next chapter he argued that syllogistic inference is pseudo, and not real inference, he here rejected the claims of the dictum because, understood in this extensional sense (the only possible interpretation according to Mill), it would exhibit syllogistic inference as 'solemn trifling'. In its place, Mill advanced two principles, one for affirmative, the other for negative syllogisms, namely: 'Things which co-exist with the same thing, co-exist with one another: or ... a thing which co-exists with another thing, which other co-exists with a third thing, also co-exists with that

23

third thing', 'A thing which co-exists with another thing, with which other a third thing does not co-exist, is not co-existent with that third thing'. (*Logic*, II, 2, 3). As R. Jackson has argued in *An Examination of the Deductive Logic of John Stuart Mill*, literally interpreted these are neither the principles of the syllogism nor true statements. Mill later advanced yet another principle which he wrongly identified with these, and wrongly claimed both to be true and to be the principle of the syllogism: 'Whatever has any mark, has that which it is a mark of. Or when the minor premise as well as the major is universal, we may state it thus: Whatever is a mark of any mark, is a mark of that which this last is a mark of' (*Logic*, II, 2, 4). Mill here saw a real problem but failed to provide a satisfactory solution; it is a problem which continues to concern logicians, some seeking the solution by reinterpreting the *dictum de omni et nullo*, others in terms of a more general principle covering deductive inference in general, and others in yet other ways.

Deductive Inference as Inference

Against the traditional view that valid syllogistic arguments yield and have yielded a vast amount of important new knowledge, Mill restated the old criticism, that inherent in all syllogistic arguments as proofs of their conclusions there is a *petitio principii*, that in all syllogisms there is a premiss which is a universal proposition that cannot be proved to be true, without first proving the conclusion to be true. When the syllogism is used to prove a conclusion, that conclusion cannot be known to be true; hence, argued Mill, the universal proposition constituting the major premiss cannot have been known to be true; yet, in advancing it as a premiss we are claiming to know it to be true. Thus Mill concluded that syllogistic arguments advanced as proofs always beg the question and can never advance our knowledge; instead, he saw the major premiss and the syllogism in general as the register or memorandum of our knowledge derived from induction. He did not dismiss the syllogism as worthless, only as worthless as proof:

It must be granted that in every syllogism, considered as an argument to prove the conclusion, there is a *petitio principii*. When we say, All men are mortal, Socrates is a man, therefore Socrates is mortal; it is unanswerably urged by the adversaries of the syllogistic theory, that the proposition, Socrates is mortal, is presupposed in the more general assumption, All men are mortal: that we cannot be assured of the mortality of all men, unless we are already certain of the mortality of every individual man: that if it be still doubtful whether Socrates, or any other individual we choose to name, be mortal or not, the same degree of uncertainty must hang over the assertion. All men are mortal: that the general principle, instead of being given as evidence of the particular case cannot itself be taken for true without exception, until every shadow of doubt which could affect any case compromised with it, is dispelled by evidence *aliundè*; and then what remains for the syllogism to prove? That, in short, no reasoning from generals to particulars can, as such, prove anything, since from a general principle we cannot infer any particulars, but those which the principle itself assumes as known. (*Logic*, II, 3, 2)

In brief, Mill argued that all real inference is inductive inference, from particulars to particulars and to generals, that the assertion of the major premiss as a step towards proving the conclusion begs the question, and that the move from the major premiss to the conclusion is in effect a form of immediate, i.e. apparent, inference. Mill's argument turns on his account of the major premiss and how it is established as true; it holds only if either the major premiss is to be interpreted enumeratively, in extension, as a shorthand statement of the indefinite number of particular statements about members of the class referred to in its subject, or if the major premiss is to be interpreted in comprehension, but to be such that it can be established only by complete enumeration. Thus, for Mill's argument to hold, the major premiss 'All men are mortal' must either be a summary way of asserting 'Socrates, Plato, Aristotle, the Duke of Wellington, etc., are mortal', or it must be such as to admit of being established only by showing that each and every man, past, present and future, is mortal. Neither alternative was open to Mill. He argued that universal propositions should be interpreted in intension or comprehension, not in extension – consider the *Logic*, 1, 5, 4, and *Hamilton*, chap. 22. Similarly, Mill could neither reasonably or consistently argue that such universal propositions can be established only by complete enumeration, since they relate to open, indefinitely large classes to which this method is inapplicable. Mill himself, in his discussion of inductive methods, argued that universal causal propositions can be proved without each member of the class involved being examined. Again, where induction provides grounds only for asserting probability and not certainty, the modal syllogism with the premiss 'All A's are probably B's' need not beg the question.

Other objections are possible. The major premiss may be an analytic proposition, yet unless the predicate is the sole identifying mark of the subject, the syllogism will not beg the question. Other universal truths, as H. W. B. Joseph and J. D. Mabbott have noted, rest on the acceptance of an authority, an expert, one's memory, the law. (See respectively *An Introduction to Logic*, pp. 301–10, 'Two Notes on Syllogism'; *Mind*, XLVIII (1939), esp. 326–34.) These too may be used as major premisses without begging the question. Thus if the university statistician records that no woman failed logic in 1968, we are entitled to infer that Jill, who sat for logic that year, passed. If the law declares it an offence to exceed 35 m.p.h. in the city, and Smith drives at 40 m.p.h. in Lygon Street, it can be inferred without committing a *petitio* that Smith has committed an offence. Even when relying on memory, e.g. having established a conclusion by complete enumeration, we may engage in a genuine inference from the universal truth concerned, e.g. that one's tan socks are whole, since all one's socks are free of holes. Mill noted these types of syllogisms and argued that 'when the premises are given by authority, the function of Reasoning is to ascertain the testimony of a witness, or the will of a legislator, by interpreting the signs in which the one has intimated his assertion and the other his command', and that 'all that we infer from the memorandum is our own previous belief (or that of those who transmitted to us the proposition) concerning the inferences which that former would warrant' (*Logic*, II, 3, 4). Mill here misdescribed the processes of reasoning cited. Other syllogisms have as major premisses those arrived at by deduction from other universal propositions; if the foregoing arguments are sound, they too would be free of the charge of *petitio principii*.

If there are synthetic *a priori* truths, syllogisms using them as major premisses would not beg the question, for the universality and necessity of such propositions is claimed to be apprehended by considering one or few cases. Thus it has been argued that reflection about pleasure, and not empirical research into all instances of pleasure, leads to awareness of the truth that pleasure as such is good; similarly with non-moral propositions such as that every event must have a cause. Mill denied that there are such propositions, resting his case chiefly on an examination of claims that certain propositions must be accepted because it is inconceivable that they be false, and on the many false claims to such knowledge in the past. Thus Mill rightly noted that Hamilton confused three distinct senses of inconceivable: meaningless or self-contradictory, incredible and inexplicable. For it to be inconceivable that a proposition be false in any one of these senses does nothing to show that it is a synthetic *a priori* truth; Mill was right to reject this argument, but it does not follow that he was right to reject the claim that synthetic *a priori* knowledge is possible. Later it will be suggested that Mill's confidence in inductive inference as based on a belief in universal causality, to be justified, involves a belief in the synthetic *a priori* character of the causal principle, and this in spite of his explicit repudiation of this view.

In brief, a person pressing a syllogistic proof may first have examined all the particulars, including that mentioned in the conclusion, and yet advance a proof which does not beg the question; and second and more importantly, the major premiss may be known independently of the particulars to which it relates and again a proof not involving a *petitio principii* is possible. Mill's error seems to have been at least in part due to his confusing the above contention with the very different one, that the addition of the universal proposition to an argument does not strengthen the argument, that to argue from 'All men to date have been mortal' to 'All men are mortal' and thence to 'The Duke of Wellington is mortal' is in no way logically stronger than to argue simply from 'All men to date have been mortal' to 'The Duke of Wellington is mortal'. This may well be true of this particular argument, even though it is not true of all deductive arguments. Further, it is a distinct contention from that, that the syllogism, when used as proof, involves the fallacy of *petitio principii*.

Mill's criticism of the use of the major premiss and the syllogism in proofs left him with the problem of explaining their importance. Here he argued that 'the major is an affirmation of the sufficiency of the evidence', that it is 'a memorandum of previous inductions', and that the syllogistic form is 'a collateral security' for the correctness of the generalisation. His comment, that in a syllogism the conclusion is drawn 'according to the formula' (*Logic*, II, 3, 4), might suggest the view that the major premiss is an inference licence or warrant which entitles us to move from particulars to particulars. This was not his view, for he accorded the major premiss no role in or behind the inference; the inference is said in no way to involve it.

Although aware of the certainty attributed to mathematical truths, and familiar with the claims that they are analytic or synthetic *a priori* truths, Mill was sufficiently extreme an empiricist to seek to explain mathematical truths as inductive truths, and the certainty attributed to them as illusory. This was consistent with his attempt to explain syllogistic reasoning as either involving the *petitio principii* or as basically (disguised) inductive reasoning, and with his attempt to explain the laws of thought as also inductive truths. Mill's detailed defence related to Euclidean geometry and arithmetic, but his contention was explicitly directed at all mathematics.

A widely held view today is that mathematics is a set of closed formal systems of analytic truths, and that its certainty comes from this fact, namely that it is necessary only to understand the meanings of the terms involved to become able to apprehend the necessity of the truths. Consider the axioms, definitions and theorems of Euclidean geometry. We teach geometry using visual illustrations as approximations to bring out the analytic truths, and not by seeking to show that they hold of physical objects. This is far from a universally held view today, as is apparent from W. V. Quine's attempt to deny the analytic–synthetic distinction, with the implied committal to a view of mathematics other than this. (See 'Two Dogmas of Empiricism', *Philosophical Review*, LX (1951).) It is, in any case, a view which encounters formidable difficulties; for example, that of explaining the relevance and utility of such formal systems with competing claims to relevance and utility, and, more generally, why it is that we need to invoke mathematical truths in so many areas and aspects of our lives, if they are simply analytic truths, truths which hold as parts of abstract formal systems, not as factual truths concerning the world.

Mill's approach was the radical one of declaring arithmetic, algebra and geometry, and indeed the basic laws of thought as well, to be well-founded generalisations, *in so far as they had any basis in truth*. His problem then became, in so far as he adhered to this approach (other views are to be found in his writings; see R. P. Anschutz, *The Philosophy of J. S. Mill*, chap. 9), that of explaining how they came to be so well established, so certain, so relevant. He set out his view concerning mathematical propositions thus:

> Now we have pointed out that, from a definition as such, no proposition, unless it be one concerning the meaning of a word, can ever follow; and that what apparently follows from a definition, follows in reality from an implied assumption that there exists a real thing conformable thereto. This assumption in the case of definitions of geometry, is not strictly true: there exist no real things exactly conformable to the definitions.... Our idea of a point I apprehend to be simply our idea of the *minimum visible*, the smallest portion of a surface which we can see. A line as defined by geometers is wholly inconceivable.... Since, then, neither in nature nor in the human mind, do there exist any objects exactly corresponding to the definitions of geometry, while yet that science cannot be supposed to be conversant about non-entities; nothing remains but to consider geometry as conversant with such lines, angles, and figures as really exist; and the definitions, as they are called, must be regarded as some of our first and most obvious generalisations concerning those natural objects. (*Logic*, II, 5, 1)

> While the axioms of demonstrative sciences thus appeared to be experimental truths, the definitions, as they are incorrectly called, in those sciences, were found by us to be generalisations from experience which are not even, accurately speaking, truths; being propositions in which, while we assert of some kind of object some property or properties which observation shows to belong to it, we at the same time deny that it possesses other properties, though in truth other properties do in every individual in-

stance accompany, and in almost all instances modify, the property thus exclusively predicated. The denial, therefore, is a mere fiction or supposition, made for the purpose of excluding the consideration of those modifying circumstances, when their influence is of too trifling amount to be worth considering. (*Logic*, ii, 6, 1)

All numbers must be numbers of something; there are no such things as numbers in the abstract. *Ten* must mean ten bodies, or ten sounds, or ten beatings of the pulse. But though numbers must be numbers of something, they may be numbers of anything.... Algebra extends the generalisation still farther: every number represents that particular number of all things without distinction, but every algebraic symbol does more, it represents all numbers without distinction.... The proposition $2(a + b) = 2a + 2b$, is a truth co-extensive with all nature. Since then algebraic truths are true of all things whatever, and not, like those of geometry, true of lines only or of angles only, it is no wonder that the symbols should not excite in our minds ideas of any things in particular.... The fundamental truths of that science [arithmetic] all rest on the evidence of sense; they are proved by showing to our eyes and our fingers that any given number of objects, ten balls, for example, may by separation and rearrangement exhibit to our senses all the different sets of numbers the sum of which is equal to ten. (*Logic*, ii, 6, 2)

These axioms, and likewise the so-called definitions [of arithmetic], are, as has already been said, results of induction; true of all objects whatever, and, as it may seem, exactly true, without the hypothetical assumption of unqualified truth where an approximation to it is all that exists. The conclusions, therefore, it will naturally be inferred, are exactly true, and the science of numbers is an exception to other demonstrative sciences in this, that the categorical certainty which is predicable of its demonstrations, is independent of all hypotheses.... Even in this case, there is one hypothetical element in the ratiocination. In all propositions concerning numbers, a condition is implied, without which none of them would be true; and that condition is an assumption which may be false. The condition is, that $1 = 1$; that all numbers are numbers of the same or of equal units. (*Logic*, II, 6, 3)

Three distinct accounts of mathematical definitions emerge in these statements. First, there is the view that a definition is an analytic, verbal proposition setting out the meanings of names and from which no facts about the world can be deduced. (This is not his considered view.) Second, definitions in arithmetic are explained as true, those of geometry as false empirical generalisations. Third, following Dugald Stewart, Mill suggested that the definitions are to be construed either as hypotheses from which deductions may be drawn, or as being true hypothetical, empirical propositions in which the antecedent, sometimes in arithmetical, always in geometrical propositions, is false. (Mill is vague in his accounts of the hypothetical character of geometrical definitions.) The hypothetical element seems to consist either in assuming that lines, angles, points, etc., exist, or in assuming that actual lines, etc., which exist, are really as the definitions explain them. Mill argued that axioms are empirical truths even though an axiom such as that two straight lines cannot enclose a space refers to lines understood as in the definition of line. Mill saw as his major opponents not those who held mathematics to be a system or systems of analytic truths, but Intuitionists such as Whewell who sought to explain mathematical propositions as factual, synthetic *a priori* truths.

Were definitions in arithmetic and geometry simply empirical generalisations as Mill suggested, it would be reasonable to investigate whether one is always one (bacteria might create problems for Mill here), and whether all triangles are in fact three-sided closed-plane figures, whether there are bent straight lines, points with size, etc. The suggestion that the definitions are hypotheses also implies the possibility and importance of similar investigations. Similarly with axioms: research directed at exhaustively testing whether two straight lines have ever enclosed a space would be reasonable. So too empirical findings concerning the sum of interior angles of a triangle, the areas of squares and circles, etc., would be important, worthwhile research comparable with that which bore on the soundness of the Newtonian Laws of Motion. The possibility of discovering phenomena which forced us to accept $2 + 2 = 5$ (in this or that context or more generally), that a circle could also be a square, etc., could not be ruled out. Further, in terms of Mill's correct insistence that inductions are reliable only within the limits of our experience, it would be unreasonable to claim that the laws of mathematics must apply to the remoter parts of the universe beyond the range of our experience. This is a radical position, and one which stems from Mill's concern to give an empiricist account of the relevance and utility of mathematics.

More serious objections are those of Frege. Frege took Mill to task for his proposed definition of 3 as $\overset{\circ\ \circ}{\circ}$ as o o o, pointing out that if arithmetic and its propositions were really a matter of rearranging physical objects, they then could not apply to strokes of a clock, to three different tastes (sweet, sour, bitter), nor to three methods of solving an equation. More basically he objected that 'Mill always confuses the applications that can be made of an arithmetical proposition, which often are physical and do presuppose observed facts, with the pure mathematical proposition itself' (*Foundations of Arithmetic*, p. 13e). The confusion is serious, for the practical applications presuppose the abstract principle. Mill in effect conceded this when he argued, in the passage quoted above, that arithmetic holds as a set of empirical truths only provided the condition $1 = 1$ is met. This same confusion led Mill to suppose that one could generalise from experience and thereby confirm or refute laws of thought

33

such as non-contradiction and excluded middle, when the very activity of generalising and confirming or refuting presuppose these laws as non-empirical truths. It might be argued that the hypothetical interpretations of the definitions of geometry are not exposed to this objection. This is true; however, they are open to the related objection that Mill has first to explain the meaningfulness of the definitions as they are literally stated in order to give meaning to his hypothetical statements or hypotheses. Any empirical account is parasitic on a non-empirical account of the meaningfulness of the definitions. Further, if mathematical propositions are taken to be empirical, they must be seen to be empirically false. Mill saw this concerning geometrical propositions and hence, in some contexts, treated them as approximate truths. However, arithmetical propositions are also empirically false if taken as empirical generalisations: two volumes plus two volumes of a gas need not always equal four volumes. That we do not modify our mathematical propositions in the way we do our empirical generalisations in the light of such counter-cases casts doubt on the empirical interpretation.

The difficulty of Mill's position is evident from his awkward handling of the axiom 'Two straight lines cannot enclose a space'. How could this impossibility be empirically established, given the unlimited length of lines? Mill resorted to the desperate, illegitimate expedient of counting as real experience imagined experiences relating to straight lines. Imagined experience is not experience, but Mill, in his appeal to it, revealed how the analytic truths of the definitions of geometry are assumed and accepted as such when applying and apparently checking the axioms which follow from them. After stressing our capacity imaginatively to represent to ourselves all possible combinations of lines and angles, and hence *imaginatively to experiment*, Mill concluded: 'Now, whether we fix our contemplation upon this imaginary picture, or call to mind the generalisations we have had occasion to make from former ocular observation, we learn by the evidence of experience, that a line which, after diverging from another straight line, begins to approach it, produces the impression on our senses which we describe by the expression, "a bent line", not by the expression, "a straight line" ' (*Logic*, II, 5, 5).

All accounts of the logical status of mathematical propositions encounter difficulties, whether they be in terms of empirical generalisations, hypothetical truths, analytic propositions, synthetic *a priori* truths or statements about ideal standards (Platonic forms) to which things in the world approximate, for a satisfactory account has to explain the relevance, utility and peculiar certainty to be attributed to mathematical propositions, different difficulties arising for different accounts.

Induction

In his treatment of induction, Mill drew heavily on the writings of his predecessors and contemporaries, especially Bacon, Hume, Herschell and Whewell. He explained induction as a process of inference which consisted in the operation of discovering and proving general propositions, as the 'process by which we conclude that what is true of certain individuals of a class is true of the whole class, or that what is true at certain times will be true in similar circumstances at all times' (*Logic*, III, 2, 1). Mill's insistence that inductive inference is real inference led him to dismiss complete enumeration as not real inductive inference; he regarded simple enumeration, i.e. induction by way of generalising from a wide and varied sample of the phenomena under investigation, to be a precarious method, although not without value; he attached less importance to the hypothetical method, of formulating hypotheses to explain and predict the facts and testing them thereby, than have most logicians, W. S. Jevons, for example, speaking of induction as consisting in 'the marriage of hypothesis and experiment' (*The Principles of Science*, esp. bk IV, chap. 23). while Whewell had been even more emphatic about its value. Mill, by contrast, simply acknowledged its utility as a method of discovery, while denying its soundness as a method of *proof*. Seeing induction as chiefly a search for causes, Mill saw the major problem as that of setting out methods of discovering and proving causal connections.

Mill believed himself to have discovered such causal methods in his so-called Four Methods (five in all), these being:

Method of Agreement. 'If two or more instances of the phenomenon under investigation have only one circumstance in common, the circumstance in which alone all the instances agree is the cause (or effect) of the given phenomenon.' (Mill symbolised this method thus: $ABC - abc, ADE - ade, A - a$.)

Method of Difference. 'If an instance in which the phenomenon under investigation occurs, and an instance in which it does not occur, have every circumstance in common save one, that one occurring only in the former; the circumstance in which alone the two instances differ is the effect, or the cause, or an indispensable part of the cause, of the phenomenon.' ($ABC - abc, BC - bc, A - a$.)

Joint Method. 'If two or more instances in which the phenomenon occurs have only one circumstance in common, while two or more instances in which it does not occur have nothing in common save the absence of that circumstance, the circumstance in which alone the two sets of instances differ is the effect, or the cause, or an indispensable part of the cause, of the phenomenon.' ($ABC - abc, ADE - ade; \bar{A}BC - \bar{a}bc, \bar{A}DE - \bar{a}de$.)

Method of Residues. 'Subduct from any phenomenon such part as is known by previous inductions to be the effect of certain antecedents, and the residues of the phenomenon is the effect of the remaining antecedents.' ($ABC - abc, BC - bc, A - a$.)

Method of Concomitant Variations. 'Whatever phenomenon varies in any manner whenever another phenomenon varies in some particular manner, is either a cause or an effect of that phenomenon, or is connected with it through some fact of causation.'

36

($A'BC - a'bc$, $A''BC - a''bc$, $A'''BC - a'''bc$.) (*Logic*, III, 8)

Most inductive logicians, in their textbooks, discuss these methods; many claim them to be of little value, but few feel free completely to ignore them. They impress the layman as little more than rigorous formulations of aspects of commonsense methods employed in everyday causal investigations. Mill advanced these Four Methods, as both Methods of discovery and Proof, as aids to the discovery of uniformities not immediately apparent and as methods of proving that the uniformities hold universally. He observed: 'The business of Inductive Logic is to provide rules and models, (such as the syllogism and its rules are for ratiocination,) to which, if inductive arguments conform, those arguments are conclusive, and not otherwise. This is what the Four Methods profess to be, and what I believe they are universally considered to be by experimental philosophers, who had practised them long before anyone sought to reduce the practice to theory' (*Logic*, III, 9, 6). Mill also claimed that these 'four methods ... are the only possible modes of experimental inquiry – of direct induction *a posteriori*, as distinguished from deduction: at least, I know not, nor am able to imagine any others' (*Logic*, III, 8, 7). To assess these Methods, they being methods of discovering and proving causal connections, Mill's account of the concept of cause needs first to be examined with a view to determining how his methods mesh in with his analysis, and whether, in the light of it, he was justified in attributing to causal, by contrast with non-causal, generalisations the great superiority he did.

Mill's Analysis of Cause

Mill's analysis of cause was firmly in the empiricist tradition and heavily indebted to that of Hume, even though it differed from the latter in significant respects, the most important being that Mill saw the cause as simply a sufficient condition, Hume as a necessary and sufficient condition. (See H. L. A. Hart and A. M. Honoré, *Causation in the Law*, chap. 1, s. ii.) Mill rejected the Intuitionist view of the causal principle as a synthetic *a priori* proposition and, following Hume, sought to explain causality in terms of observable relations. Mill explained the cause as the antecedent, the effect as the invariable consequent, invariable sequence being the core of his account. His view of the cause as a/the sufficient condition was explained, in spite of careless statements to the contrary in terms of the cause, as 'the antecedent which is invariably followed by the consequent', not as the antecedent which invariably precedes the consequent. The cause was construed by him as 'the whole of the contingencies of every description, which being realised, the consequent invariably follows'. (*See Logic*, III, 5, 2 and 3.) Mill elsewhere explained causality in terms of unconditional, invariable sequence, unconditionality relating to the absence of counteracting causes. While the inclusion of this element in Mill's analysis complicates any statement concerning causes of phenomena (we should rarely be able to indicate any), it is vital if Mill is to explain causality in terms of the empirically observable, invariable sequence he indicated, for otherwise counteracting causes would render the sequences variable. (The alternative move, and one commonly adopted today, is to include a reference to standing conditions; such a move, for reasons which will be apparent in Chapter 5, would create difficulties in the defence of phenomenalism. None the less in Book VI he does seem to have suggested some such amendment.) Mill further thought that the reference to unconditionalness would help him to explain what was true in the claim that causal connections are necessary connections. Here he wrote:

Invariable sequence, therefore, is not synonymous with causation, unless the sequence, besides being invariable, is unconditional. There are sequences, as uniform in past experience as any others whatever,

38

which yet we do not regard as cases of causation, but as conjunctions in some sort accidental.... We may define, therefore, the cause of a phenomenon to be the antecedent or the concurrence of antecedents, on which it is invariably and *unconditionally* conseequent. Or if we adopt the convenient modification of the meaning of the word 'cause', which confines it to the assemblage of positive conditions without the negative, then instead of 'unconditionally' we must say 'subject to no other than negative conditions'. (*Logic*, III, 5, 6)

Important though it is for his empiricist, reductionist analysis, Mill's inclusion of unconditionalness or absence of counteracting causes in his concept of cause results in difficulties. As Joseph has argued, if the cause is the antecedent in an unconditional, invariable sequence, the counteracting cause will be the antecedent after which the consequent invariably does not follow, except when counteracting causes of the counteracting cause occur. Using such a definition with ingenuity, quite different combinations of antecedents, counteracting causes (other antecedents) and counter-counteracting causes (other antecedents again) could be indicated as the cause. Secondly, Mill's account involves a significant revision of ordinary causal language, according to which we now speak of causes being prevented from achieving their effects, of conditional causal laws, laws of tendencies, etc. (Mill himself failed to adhere consistently to his usage, coming to speak of laws of tendencies.) The notion of a counteracting cause as now understood would have to be abandoned. Further, all causal statements would be incomplete and provisional until the impossible was achieved, namely all causes including counteracting causes were discovered. The mere complexity of causes renders the project of discovering causes, on Mill's account of 'cause', empirically impossible. In any ordinary sense of 'cause', we can and do discover causes. The linguistic revision Mill's account involves is of little moment, but it does bring out that Mill's concept

39

is not the ordinary concept and that the account he offered is not what is ordinarily meant by 'cause'.

The reference to unconditionality was also thought, by Mill, to explain the apparent necessity of causal invariable sequences. It does not do this. We do not need to discover that a sequence is invariable to know that it is a causal one; rather we infer the former from the latter. This happens when we draw a conclusion using the method of difference. This would not be so if, to discover that A is a cause, we needed to discover that there is an invariable sequence. Further, there is no paradox in asserting that a sequence is an invariable, merely contingent, non-causal one. On Mill's analysis a self-contradiction would be involved in such a statement. These considerations point towards an account of causal sequences in terms of connections, the cause being related to the effect in more than a purely contingent, temporal relationship.

The concept of cause noted above is not the only one with which Mill operated. As Joseph noted, permanent causes such as gravity do not lend themselves easily to analysis as antecedents invariably followed by their consequents. Further, the sense in which hydrogen and oxygen might be said to be causes of water, or that the nature of the surface of mother-of-pearl is the cause of its appearance, would seem to be different from this invariable sequence sense of cause. Mill seemed, in fact, to have operated with a variety of concepts when explaining and illustrating his Four Methods, some of them being unanalysed.

The Four Methods of Experimental Inquiry

Mill was a careless writer; this is nowhere more evident than in his discussion of his Methods. He entitled his chapter 'Of the Four Methods...' and offered his reader five, where there is room for debate concerning which is not of the four. Further, both in introducing and in summing up his conclusions, Mill emphasised that they were methods of proof, yet in the detailed discussion of them he repeatedly acknowledged that the Method of Agreement cannot give proof. None the less the methods are of importance as aids to the discovery of causes and as means of checking the soundness of causal generalisations. Their value may now usefully be considered. (See statements of the methods, p. 36.)

1. *Agreement*. This method consists in comparing instances of a phenomenon, the cause or effect of which we wish to discover, and eliminating all the antecedents not present on every occasion on which the phenomenon occurs. It is claimed to be of value where only observation is possible. Examples would be: comparing antecedents in an outbreak of typhoid and finding only the one common antecedent, the drinking of milk from the one dairy; the attributing to the only common antecedent, frost, the withering of flowers.

2. *Difference*. This is the method of artificial experiment, it being the nature of a controlled experiment to introduce into the pre-existing state of circumstances a definite change. Examples include Newton's guinea and feather experiment to show the effect of air on the rate of fall of bodies, and Mill's example of plunging a bird into carbon dioxide, thereby causing its death, carbon dioxide being seen to be the cause of its death.

3. *The Joint Method of Agreement and Difference, the Indirect Method of Difference, the Double Employment of the Method of Agreement*. As the various names suggest, this method involves comparing cases in which the phenomenon occurs and noting the antecedent (or consequent), and comparing cases in which it does not occur. Examples here include experiments with a control group, e.g. those with rats which suggested that acquired characteristics are not inherited.

4. *Residues*. This is a special application of the method of difference. By seeking an explanation of the perturbation of Uranus, Neptune was discovered.

5. *Concomitant Variations*. This is the method of correlations, of observing parallel variations in phenomena. Examples include the relating the occurrence of tides with the movements of the moon, the variations in movements of pendulums with the earth's

gravity, etc. This method is claimed to have special value because of the immovable, permanent causes, and as one which can make more precise certain causal relationships discovered by the method of difference.

Other Methods

Although Mill claimed the Four Methods to be the totality of inductive methods, in Book VI, when discussing methods in the social sciences, he dismissed these methods and noted and considered a number of others. Among these, he rejected the Chemical or Experimental Method (i.e. the above methods) as inapplicable, and the Geometrical Method (as proceeding on a false assumption that there is only one causal factor operating in these areas); the Deductive or Concrete Deductive Method, the Inverse Deductive Method (for which he was indebted to Comte) and the Hypothetical Method were accepted as of value, Mill seeing the former two as ways of employing the Four Methods. In fact they are as distinctly different from the basic three as are the Joint Method and the Method of Residues, and while they involve the use of the Four Methods, they are themselves not basically methods of elimination as are the Four Methods.

The Deductive or Concrete Deductive Method consists in determining the laws of separate causes using the Four Methods, reasoning from the simple laws to complex cases, and verifying the deduction by reference to experience. This, Mill observed, is the method used in astronomy. *The Inverse Deductive Method* involves observing uniformities in nature, e.g. from a study of history, and inferring them back to known psychological causal laws. This method Mill thought to be most appropriate in the social sciences where, he claimed, the Four Methods do not admit of application owing to the facts of plurality of causes, intermixture of effects, and the impossibility of experiments. *The Hypothetical Method* and *Argument by Analogy* (*Logic*, III, 14 and 20) are seen by Mill to be closely related, arguments by analogy suggesting hypotheses. Mill construed the hypothetical method and argument by analogy (which he appears to have treated as a special case of it) as useful as methods of discovery but as failing as methods of proof. Successfully to explain and even to predict the facts according to Mill and as against Whewell is not to prove the hypothesis, for more than one hypothesis may do this. Mill further proposed to limit the 'scientific' use of the hypothetical method to hypotheses which postulate only entities which admit of empirical verification. However, Mill was vague and uncritical concerning what counted as empirical verification, and allowed as genuine scientific hypotheses, theories, laws, those concerning light, Newton's laws, psychological laws, i.e. hypotheses which involve reference to unobservable phenomena such as luminiferous ether, force, ideas, etc.

As methods of inductive discovery, seven of the eight methods, the exception being the hypothetical method, suffer from the limitation of being simply methods of discovering *causal* generalisations; hence they need to be supplemented by methods such as those of simple and complete enumeration. Indeed, as will be argued later, for Mill they derive their cogency from their dependence on the method of simple enumeration. Mill overestimated the role of discovering causal connections (the theoretical sciences use causal expressions much less than might be supposed) and underestimated the importance of the hypothetical method, the only one of his methods of value in non-causal inquiries. He also owing, no doubt, to his preoccupation with proof failed to appreciate the scope and range of useful hypotheses, not all useful scientific hypotheses being such as to admit of direct empirical verification in respect of their constituent elements.

Only three of the five Four Methods are basic methods, and even these – Agreement, Difference and Concomitant Variations – are not the bedrock and only such methods as Mill's comments would suggest. Their use to make discoveries presupposes much knowledge derived from other methods or from cruder uses

43

of themselves, on the basis of which hypotheses may be formulated and used in combination with them. Mill's examples reveal this, although his symbolism, grossly oversimplified as it is, obscures how extensive is the knowledge presupposed. If it is considered how one, possessed of no knowledge of likely causes, might attempt to apply Mill's methods to discover the cause of the common cold, or of baldness, it is evident how important are both the background knowledge and the hypotheses based on it. Mill did acknowledge the utility of applying his methods on the basis of hypotheses concerning the probable cause, but failed to appreciate the inductive significance of the work involved in arriving at these hypotheses. Much of the important work of science is done here, and far too little was said by Mill concerning the problem of arriving at useful hypotheses to test by the use of his methods. Part of this criticism is that concerning the dependence of the methods on a prior judgement of relevance. Even where an hypothesis is not formulated and tested by the methods, there must at least be a judgement concerning the factors which are relevant; if that judgement is wrongly made, the methods may fail to discover the cause and even lead to mistaken conclusions. Textbook examples are misleading because they illustrate the methods as operating only after such judgements of relevance have been made. Many great advances in science have come from an awareness that factors deemed remote and irrelevant – e.g. activity of sunspots in respect of weather – are very relevant. The methods may themselves be used in rough and ready ways to suggest which factors are relevant, but the major judgements of relevance are made by way of hypotheses of very general kinds. This is evident from the fact that an aspect of this criticism concerning the judgement of relevance is the fact that the methods can be applied only after the situation being investigated has been analysed; how it is analysed may seriously influence the conclusion to which the methods lead.

Although Mill offered an analysis of cause which involved as part of its definition that its effect invariably follows it, in discussing the Four Methods he treated as a problem for them the fact he described as 'the intermixture of effects'—

> A concurrence of two or more causes, not separately producing each its own effect, but interfering with or modifying the effects of one another, takes place, as has already been explained, in two different ways. In the one which is exemplified by the joint operation of different forces in mechanics, the separate effects of all the causes continue to be produced, but are compounded with one another, and disappear in one total. In the other, illustrated by the case of chemical action, the separate effects cease entirely, and are succeeded by phenomena altogether different, and are governed by different laws. (*Logic*, III, 10, 4)

Admission of the phenomenon of intermixture of effects involves Mill in rejecting his account of cause as the antecedent invariably and unconditionally followed by the effect in favour of a view of cause as what *would be* a sufficient condition in the absence of counteracting causes (there are obvious difficulties here), or as a necessary condition for the occurrence of the event. This uncertainty concerning Mill's concept here makes it difficult to assess the implications of the problem of the intermixture of effects on the utility and reliability of the methods, although it is obviously relevant to the claims of the methods of difference, residues and concomitant variations as methods of discovery and proof. Consider where poison and its antidote have been administered.

A general, and also a specific, ground for questioning Mill's claim that his methods provide proof may now be considered. Firstly, Mill's methods are methods of elimination; as such they are open to error and do not admit of the certainty Mill claimed on their behalf. (The eliminating of alternatives is distinct from attempting to falsify an hypothesis.) Secondly, more specifically, they may lead to false conclusions. Mill himself noted that the fact of plurality of causes may lead to false or misleading conclusions. Events and phenomena such as outbreaks of typhoid, expansion of gases, death, fires, divorce, economic crises, wars, evidently result from many causes. Any method of proving causal connections, which proceeded on the assumption that there was only one cause (for Mill, one sufficient condition) for each event or phenomenon, would lead to at least some false conclusions. It is sometimes argued that there is only one cause for each event. This is true if cause and event are appropriately defined (the latter as being unique). It is implausible if cause is defined as by Mill and if it is types of events which are being investigated. Mill and the scientist are primarily interested in discovering not causes of unique events but causes of types of events, hence Mill's problem of the plurality of causes. The latter fact renders the method of agreement unreliable – it may suggest that there is no cause (e.g. where there is no common antecedent), or an irrelevant factor may be deemed the cause. The latter could also occur with the method of concomitant variations, where there is the added uncertainty due to the phenomenon of 'the intermixture of effects'. Alternatively, a number of sufficient conditions, ABC, ADE, may be rejected as not the cause, in favour of part of the sufficient conditions A, where A need not be a necessary condition. The method of difference is not exposed to this difficulty, but the fact of plurality of causes none the less weakens the conclusions which can legitimately be drawn from it, the only legitimate conclusion being that where a follows the introduction of A, A may be said to be either a or the sufficient condition or part of a sufficient condition of a. There are other sources of error with the methods of difference and residues. As the history of science reveals, the wrong conclusion may result because unnoticed factors are introduced (or present, with residues). Consider experiments relating to diseases before the discovery of bacteria. The use of the Joint method may lessen the risk of error, but not completely eliminate it. Further, the fact of intermixture of effects may lead to false conclusions, as when an unknown counteracting cause is present. Thus, separately and together, the Four Methods may lead to false conclusions, and hence cannot be methods of proof. Mill none the less persisted in describing them as such.

In Book VI, chap. 6 of the *Logic* Mill surprisingly argued that the Four Methods are inapplicable in the social sciences because of the impossibility of experiments (important controlled experiments are possible) and because of the facts of plurality of causes and interactions of causes with causes, effects with effects. These in fact are difficulties to which they are exposed in all contexts, and provided it is realised that they do not prove a generalisation, the Four Methods, especially concomitant variations, agreement, and difference, when used in conjunction with the hypothetical method, have value in the social sciences. Mill's other methods, the Concrete and Inverse Deductive Methods, also have a use, but their importance was overestimated by Mill, at least in part, because he believed it to be vital to ground social generalisations on psychological laws, and did not fully appreciate the possibility of giving causal explanations, and discovering causal laws, at different levels. Sometimes the psychological explanation of social behaviour is the most useful, illuminating, relevant one; at other times, political, economic and even chemical and physical accounts are more illuminating. Further, on Mill's view of cause, if social laws can be grounded on social evidence, there is no reason to believe them to be more strongly grounded if derived by psychological laws.

Ultimate and Derivative Laws

Mill saw the way towards establishing causal generalisations as consisting in the gathering together of empirical generalisations and lesser laws under more general laws, where one of his models was gravity and

47

the many lesser generalisations concerning objects acting under the influence of gravity. He thought of empirical laws which were not deductively connected with such basic laws as not proven, and as being only as sound as inductions by simple enumeration. In fact, if Mill's methods gave proof, many of these lesser causal generalisations would admit of proof as fully as would the ultimate laws. Further, this tracing of derivative and empirical laws to ultimate laws is not the simple thing Mill supposed it to be. Causal laws explaining human behaviour in terms of laws of motion are not reducible to more ultimate psychological laws. Both are ultimate laws in respect of much 'behaviour'. So too with other types of causal explanations. We need to examine whether the one causal explanation is or is not reducible to another type.

Mill treated causation as the core of induction, yet the word 'cause' is used relatively little in the theoretical sciences. This fact links with another. Mill treated all laws and genuinely scientific hypotheses as directly empirically confirmable in principle, and as being like generalisations of the form 'All A's are B's', or 'All X's are caused by A', where A, B and X are empirically observable. The more important, higher-level theories are very unlike empirical generalisations such as 'All crows are black'. Further, Mill wrote as if causal laws are major premises from which we deduce conclusions in the light of the observed facts, when in fact the role of laws is much more complex, it being argued by many, e.g. S. Toulmin in *The Philosophy of Science*, that scientists use laws as principles or techniques for inferring and not as generalisations. Consider the atomic theory, theories such as Boyle's Law ('The volume occupied by the same sample of any gas at constant temperature is inversely proportional to its pressure' – $PV = k$), Charles's Law, Hooke's Law, Snell's Law, or the kinetic theory of gases. These and like laws are not empirical generalisations. Apparent exceptions lead to statements about the scope of the law rather than to rejection of the law. Further, the law may refer

48

to unobservables. With higher-level theories new terms are introduced, e.g. 'refractive index', 'photon', which have meaning only in the context of the theory. Thus Mill even though he was acquainted with empirical hypotheses, theories and laws, including theories concerning light, which were in principle unprovable in respect of their details by direct empirical observation, adopted a very crude, oversimplified view of scientific theorising. This no doubt was in part due to his underestimation of the value of the hypothetical method, to his uncritical acceptance of extreme empiricism, as well as to his lack of training in the sciences. (Bain supplied many of his examples of his Methods.) Today one of the more interesting questions of philosophy consists in determining the logical and ontological status of scientific entities, i.e. entities which are introduced in scientific laws and theories. Are they real entities, although not directly observable, or are they *as if* entities, models, or simply elements of inference licences? Mill's narrow view of what it is to offer an explanation obscured from him both the importance of hypotheses and the hypothetical method, and the different levels of scientific theorising.

The Ground and Justification of Induction

Unlike many of our contemporary philosophers, Mill accepted that he was involved in explaining by what right we infer from the known to the unknown, i.e. what is the ground of induction. Mill, I suggest, was right in this, that the problem is an important one which does not admit of facile dissolution as a pseudo-problem in the ways suggested by such dissolutionists as P. Edwards and P. F. Strawson. (Edwards pressed a paradigm-case argument about 'reasons', that what we mean by good reasons includes reasons of the kinds that figure in inductive inferences; hence it is absurd to ask for good reasons for relying on reasons in inductive inferences – see P. Edwards 'Russell's Doubts about Induction', *Mind*, LVIII (1949). Strawson represented the problem as that of asking for a justification for relying on inductive procedures, they being by definition logically sound procedures – see P. F. Strawson, *Logical Theory*, chap. 9. Edwards's argument is met by distinguishing what is denoted and what connoted by a word. The problem may then be put: Given that 'good reason' has the connotation it has, are we right in including inductive reasons, i.e. those pointed to by inductive logicians, in its denotation? Strawson's claim is met by noting that what is being sought is not a justification of induction in the abstract, but of this or that inductive theory. In Mill's case, the problem was to justify relying on conclusions arrived at by his methods. Strawson's move does nothing to render Mill's problem a pseudo- and not a real one.)

Mill saw no problem in justifying induction by simple enumeration; there he appealed to the commonsense reliance on it, and seems to have supposed that, if seen to be fallible, and to give only probable conclusions, where the degree of probability is related to the range and variety of cases examined, there is no problem. This of course will not do. The problem here consists in showing that we are justified in attributing any probability to the conclusions. Attempts to justify it in terms of its past reliability commit two errors: they beg the question by seeking to use the method to justify itself, and they are unfounded, as not all past reliance on the method has been justified. There is therefore a problem with induction by simple enumeration which is all the more important as Mill sought to ground the principle of causality on it.

Mill commenced his discussion of the problem as he saw it by suggesting that induction rests on a belief in the uniformity of nature, and later implied that this principle is that of universal causation, even though he was aware of non-causal uniformities and co-existences. It is probable that in his initial discussion he had in mind a principle of the uniformity of nature which included but was not confined to the principle of universal causality, for he wrote:

We must first observe that there is a principle implied in the very statement of what Induction is; an assumption with regard to the course of nature and the order of the universe; namely, that there are such things in nature as parallel cases; that what happens once will, under a sufficient degree of similarity of circumstances, happen again, and not only again, but as often as the same circumstances recur. This, I say, is an assumption involved in every case of Induction.... The proposition that the course of nature is uniform, is the fundamental principle, or general axiom, of Induction. (*Logic*, III, 3, 1. See also III, 4, 1 and III, 5, 1.)

Some such assumption does underlie the use of inductive methods. Were there no uniformities, inductive methods as now formulated would necessarily lead to false conclusions. However, such a principle could not provide a justification of induction, for the only principle that could do that would be the true principle setting out all the actual uniformities. Mill seemed to see this when he wrote that 'the uniformity of the course of nature, is, ... itself a complex fact, compounded of all the separate uniformities which exist in respect to single phenomena' (*Logic*, III, 4, 1). Yet it is towards the discovery of these that induction is directed. To suggest that this principle could justify induction is misleading because (i) it would provide a justification only of true inductions, (ii) to say this is to say that it justifies itself, since the principle would simply be the sum of all possible true inductions, (iii) we therefore could never use it to justify any proposed inductive inference, for we could not know the principle until we first determined which inductions were true, i.e. justified. Yet surprisingly Mill spoke of such a principle as a warrant for our inductions, and as *the ultimate major premiss* of all inductions (*Logic*, III, 3, 1). In chap. 5, and in later chapters of this same Book, Mill came increasingly to treat this principle as that of universal causality. The latter principle's claim to be the ground of causal inductions at least seems less desperate than that of a law of the uniformity of nature which consists in the totality of true inductions. Mill here wrote:

> The Law of Causation, the recognition of which is the main pillar of inductive science, is but the familiar truth, that invariability of succession is found by observation to obtain between every fact in nature and some other fact which has preceded it; .... For every event there exists some combination of objects or events, some given concurrence of circumstances, positive and negative, the occurrence of which is always followed by the phenomenon.... On the universality of this truth depends the possibility of reducing the inductive process to rules. (*Logic*, III, 5, 2)

> The validity of all Inductive Methods depends on the assumption that every event, or the beginning of every phenomenon, must have some cause, some antecedent, on the existence of which it is invariably and unconditionally consequent. ... The universality of the law of causation is assumed in them all. (*Logic*, III, 21, 1)

Mill noted the instinctive nature of a belief in causal uniformity but denied that it constituted a ground for relying on it. He also rejected the Intuitionists' claims that the causal principle is self-evident, that it is inconceivable that it be false, noting that a causeless or partially causeless universe is imaginable. He then argued that the principle is established by simple enumeration of the most searching, far-reaching kind, and hence that its truth must be taken as holding only in those parts of the universe in which it has been found to hold (*Logic*, III, 21, 4). In s. 3 of this chapter, Mill noted that the precariousness of the method of simple enumeration is in an inverse ratio to the largeness of the generalisation, and hence that here it is not precarious. This contention cannot succeed. Mill claimed that whenever we look for causes, i.e. antecedents invariably and unconditionally followed by consequents, we find them – that there are no disconfirming, only a wide range of confirming, cases. In fact, unless the question is begged, and the truth of the causal principle assumed, no confirming cases can be claimed. At best, Mill's Methods provide grounds for accepting observed unvarying connections as holding; they provide no grounds for claiming to have discovered invariable sequences. Experience can never reveal a connection to be for ever invariable, hence it cannot provide the required confirming cases necessary for the use of the method of simple enumeration. Mill seemed implicity to have invoked the hypothetical method, advancing an hypothesis that invariable sequences occur, and looking and finding the anticipations of the hypothesis confirmed. Further, Mill's implied claim that there have never been disconfirming cases, that all the evidence within human experience confirms the universality of causality, is also open to question. A causeless change has never been conclusively identified, but this may simply be because it is difficult to know what would count as conclusive evidence that an event has no cause. Mill's discussion of miracles suggests that he would not have accepted anything as an uncaused event but only because of the depth of his conviction concerning the universality of causality (see chap. 6 below). Yet unless there are criteria determining what constitute disconfirming cases, such that we can investigate whether such cases occur, it cannot be claimed that there are no disconfirming cases. What is true is that there is a vast number of cases in which scientists have unsuccessfully searched for causes, quite apart from the area of human conduct; very often the search has been thorough and sustained. Were we not so deeply committed to a belief in the universality of causality we should be inclined to treat such searches as counter-instances, as we do the failure to find a black polar bear as disconfirming that there are such bears. Mill seemed vaguely aware of this, for when seeking to show that no *petitio principii* nor inconsistency was involved in using simple enumeration to prove the ground of stronger causal inferences, he argued that

53

the particular causal inferences, besides strengthening the case for the general principle, receive strength from it, for example, where the causes are uncertain:

> ... though itself obtained by induction from particular laws of causation, as not less certain, but, on the contrary, more so, than any of those from which it was drawn. It adds to them as much proof as it receives from them. For there is probably no one even of the best established laws of causation which is not sometimes counteracted, and to which, therefore, apparent exceptions do not present themselves, which would have necessarily and justly shaken the confidence of mankind in the universality of those laws, if inductive processes founded on the universal law had not enabled us to refer those exceptions to the agency of counteracting causes, and thereby reconcile them with the law with which they apparently conflict.... To the law of causation, on the contrary, we not only do not know of any exception, but the exceptions which limit or apparently invalidate the special laws, are so far from contradicting the universal one, that they confirm it; since in all cases which are sufficiently open to our observation, we are able to trace the difference of result, either to the absence of a cause which had been present in ordinary cases, or to the presence of one which had been absent. (*Logic*, III, 21, 3)

Mill here abandoned his account of cause as a sufficient condition for an unexplained notion in order to speak of causal laws which admit of exceptions due to counteracting causes. Had Mill appreciated what he was doing here, he might have reconsidered the adequacy of the empirical evidence for his induction from simple enumeration to the principle of universal causality. Further, even were this principle well supported by this method, Mill would have been entitled to attribute to causal inductions based on it not greater but less probability than is to be attributed to it, for the individual, causal inductions introduce new

54

sources of error. Yet how else could Mill have believed his Four Methods to provide proofs? Revealing that all was not well with his position, Mill argued that 'the assertion that our inductive processes assume the law of causation, while the law of causation is itself a case of induction, is a paradox, only on the old theory of reasoning, which supposes the universal truth, a major premise, in a ratiocination, to be the real proof of the particular truths which are ostensibly inferred from it'. (*Logic*, III, 21, 4.) This will not do; the Four Methods rest on the truth of universal causality and are uncertain to the extent that it is uncertain. In restricting his claim to knowledge of causality to those parts and areas of the universe with which we are familiar, Mill acknowledged this, that 'the uniformity in the succession of events, otherwise called the law of causation, must be received not as a law of the universe, but of that portion of it only which is within the range of our means of sure observation, with a reasonable degree of extension to adjacent cases'. (*Logic*, III, 21, 4.) By seeking to base most inductions on the causal principle, and the latter in turn on simple enumeration, Mill made induction stand or fall on the soundness of that method. Further, even were it to admit of justification, e.g. as a method which gave probable conclusions – and no satisfactory justification was advanced by Mill – this would not be a completely adequate ground for those inductions Mill sought to justify, for they depended also on his Four Methods. In fact, if induction is to be grounded on the causal principle, it could only satisfactorily be so grounded if the causal principle could be shown to be a synthetic *a priori* truth.

Mill's more important contributions to ethics occur in *Utilitarianism* (1863, from *Fraser's Magazine*, 1861), *Bentham* (1838), *Coleridge* (1840), *Dr Whewell on Moral Philosophy* (1852), *Professor Sedgwick's Discourse on the Studies of the University of Cambridge* (1835), and in the brief discussion in the *System of Logic*, bk VI, chap. 12. Although he was concerned to reject Intuitionism, and although in the *Logic* he noted some differences between ordinary factual statements and statements concerning obligations, Mill did not develop a meta-ethic, his major concern being, in spite of a brief, qualified anti-Benthamite period, to state and defend a utilitarian normative ethic. Estimates of the value of Mill's contributions here have varied greatly, G. E. Moore observing that 'This [*Utilitarianism*] is a book which contains an admirably clear and fair discussion of many ethical principles and methods' (*Principia Ethica*, p. 64), while more recently J. Plamenatz has expressed a much less favourable, although also widely accepted, estimate. After observing that *Liberty*, *Representative Government* and *Utilitarianism* were works of 'a sick man in his premature old age', that they exhibit all his defects, 'his lack of clarity, his inconsistency and his inability either to accept wholeheartedly or to reject the principles inherited from his father and from Bentham', and that his good qualities 'accentuate the defects', Plamenatz observed that 'the most defective of the essays is *Utilitarianism*, in which Mill seems to lose control of his arguments at every turn. It is the product of an intelligent and honest but almost exhausted mind.' Yet even he went on, surprisingly, to observe: 'For all their defects *Liberty* and *Utilitarianism* are important works' (*The English Utilitarians*, p. 123).

Mill's ethical writings are substantially attempts to defend a modified Benthamite utilitarianism against its critics. His early training and discipleship made it important to him that he defend the formal statement of Bentham's utilitarianism, even though and when, in seeking to circumvent difficulties, he either knowingly or unknowingly changed its substance, at times abandoning its hedonism, its radical practical claims, and even its claim to be the ethic binding on all peoples, of all ages. Mill could, as he claimed in his early letter to Carlyle, reasonably describe himself as a utilitarian; equally, Benthamite utilitarians could be excused for preferring the attacks of non-utilitarians to the defences and restatements offered by John Stuart Mill. Bentham had argued that the ultimate principle of morality is the greatest happiness principle, and this he applied and interpreted on the basis of a very slightly qualified psychological egoistic theory of human motivation. *Utilitarianism* can properly be construed as the transitory stage from this predominantly egoistic utilitarianism of Bentham, James Mill and their eighteenth-century precursors (Hume excepted, not being a utilitarian)[1] and the altristic utilitarianism of this, and the latter part of the nineteenth, century; this even though Mill used psychological egoistic arguments. Mill's *Utilitarianism* and *Liberty* also mark a departure from the hedonistic utilitarianism of Bentham, with its stress on pleasure and pain, towards the ideal utilitarianism of G. E. Moore, Hastings Rashdall and their followers this century, Moore and Rashdall developing Mill's implicit recognition that pleasure is not the sole good, pain not the sole evil, and that the rightness of actions turns on the goodness, and not simply the pleasure–pain content of their consequences. Further, in spite of Mill's explicit, uncom-

---

[1] Hume was primarily concerned to develop a metaethical theory in terms of the feelings/responses of the impartial spectator. He saw as virtues that which is pleasing for its own sake, that which is useful simply to its possessor, and that which is of general utility. The former two kinds of virtues need not be utilitarian virtues.

promising rejection of intuitionism, these two essays contain the seeds of a move from the anti-intuitionism of Bentham to the intuitionism of Henry Sidgwick, Moore and Rashdall. It is to the common, but not essential, intuitionist contentions, that there are many and not simply one ultimate, irreducible principle of obligation, and that the consequences, intended or actual, need not determine the morality of the action, that Mill took exception. He also hinted at another major departure from Benthamism in his account of justice, there adopting what is now known as a rule utilitarian position, that it is obligatory to conform with socially useful rules, even when the particular act in conformity with the rule leads to less general good. Again, should utilitarians resolve their problem of determining what is the true test of the rightness of the action – its actual, ascertainable, probable or intended consequences – Mill's writings, even though he generally settled for probable consequences, are rich in suggestions relevant to each possible view. So too there is the difference that Bentham's was a radical, practical theory, whereas in Mill's writings, in *Bentham* more than in *Utilitarianism*, there is a suggestion, but only a suggestion, that it be viewed as a theoretical, explanatory theory, rather than as one with direct practical implications and involving a rethinking and reassessing of conventional moral rules. Thus, if Mill's utilitarian writings are traced to their major source, they lead to one kind of theory; if the implications of Mill's qualifications are worked out in detail and full note taken of the implicit as well as explicit suggestions, we have source material from which many varieties of contemporary utilitarianism have, or could have, developed.

Mill's Defence of Utilitarianism

Mill's starting point was that 'All action is for the sake of some end, and rules of action, it seems natural to suppose, must take their whole character and colour from the end to which they are subservient' (*Utilitarianism*, Everyman ed., p. 2; all subsequent references are to this edition), and: 'That the morality of actions depends upon the consequences which they tend to produce, is the doctrine of rational persons of all schools' (*Bentham*, in *Dissertations and Discussions*, I 385–6). Mill here failed to grasp that rational beings often deem it important to act on principles irrespective of the ends to be achieved thereby, or in spite of the consequences; that it may be thought to be important to be honest, just, fair, for the sake of honesty, justice, fairness, and not for the sake of some end or ends to be achieved thereby; hence he sought to show that even Kant took note of the consequences in estimating the morality of actions. (The passage Mill referred to relates to possible, not actual, consequences.) Mill accordingly saw it as his task to show, as against the Intuitionists who discern a plurality of principles (this is not a necessary feature of intuitionism), that there is one and only one principle of morality, the principle of utility, 'that actions are right in proportion as they tend to promote happiness, wrong as they tend to produce the reverse of happiness', going on to observe here 'by happiness is intended pleasure, and the absence of pain; by unhappiness, pain and the privation of pleasure' (*Utilitarianism*, p. 6). There is little specific argument against pluralist, non-utilitarian theories, Mill simply contending that logically there must be some ultimate principle to decide between any plurality of principles. In the *Logic* he had so argued:

> There are not only first principles of Knowledge, but first principles of Conduct. There must be some standard by which to determine the goodness or badness, absolute and comparative, of ends or objects of desire. And whatever that standard is, there can be but one: for if there were several ultimate principles of conduct, the same conduct might be approved by one of those principles and condemned by another; and there would be needed

some more general principle, as umpire between them. (VI, 12, 7)

This is not so. Even a cursory glance at other areas of human choice ought to have revealed to Mill that there may be conflicting considerations relevant to choice, and no common basis for choosing between them. It is then that we speak of and engage in the process of 'weighing up' conflicting considerations. Mill here confused ultimate principles with principles of absolute obligation. As W. D. Ross brought out in *The Right and The Good*, the ultimate principles may be principles of *prima facie* or intrinsic and not of absolute obligation, and, when they are so understood, and the notion of weighing up conflicting duties, claims, considerations is properly acknowledged, it becomes evident that there need be no one single, ultimate determining principle. Thus Mill's defence of utilitarianism involves showing not simply that utility is a principle, but that it is the sole ultimate principle of morality.

Unlike some utilitarians Mill did not seek to qualify his principle of utility by reference to a principle of fairness or impartiality in the distribution of pleasure. In chap. 5 of *Utilitarianism* (p. 58) he argued that 'Everybody to count for one, nobody for more than one' is part of the principle. This is true in the sense in which Mill interpreted it, namely, as asserting that equal amounts of pleasure are to count equally. This, however, brings out how misleading the statement is. It is not asserting that humans, or humans and animals (animal pleasure enters into Mill's calculus) are to count equally, only that equal amounts of pleasure are to count equally. The principle is not one of fairness, as a literal interpretation of it may suggest. (A person may impartially but unfairly always prefer his own pleasure to that of his wife's when equal amounts are involved, on this principle.) This means that Mill was involved in establishing only the one ultimate principle, and not a second principle of fairness as well. Difficulties arise for his theory on this account which

60

will be noted later, difficulties which acceptance of the claim that to adopt utilitarianism as a morality involves impartiality in applying the principle does little to help, for this impartiality is simply consistency of the kind noted here by Mill.

Having noted that 'questions of ultimate ends are not amenable to direct proof', but that 'considerations may be presented capable of determining the intellect either to give or to withhold its assent', Mill much later on in the essay, in chap. 4, set out his proof, in this weaker sense of proof, thus:

> Questions about ends are, in other words, questions what things are desirable. The utilitarian doctrine is, that happiness is desirable, and the only thing desirable, as an end; all other things being only desirable as means to that end. What ought to be required of this doctrine – what conditions is it requisite that the doctrine should fulfil – to make good its claim to be believed?
>
> The only proof capable of being given that an object is visible, is that people actually see it. The only proof that a sound is audible, is that people hear it: and so of the other sources of our experience. In like manner, I apprehend, the sole evidence it is possible to produce that anything is desirable, is that people do actually desire it. If the end which the utilitarian doctrine proposes to itself were not, in theory and in practice, acknowledged to be an end, nothing could ever convince any person that it was so. No reason can be given why the general happiness is desirable, except that each person, so far as he believes it to be attainable, desires his own happiness. This, however, being a fact, we have not only all the proof which the case admits of, but all which it is possible to require, that happiness is a good: that each person's happiness is a good to that person, and the general happiness, therefore, a good to the aggregate of all persons. Happiness has made out its title as *one* of the ends of conduct, and consequently one of the criteria of morality.

But it has not, by this alone, proved itself to be the sole criterion. To do that, it would seem, by the same rule, necessary to show, not only that people desire happiness, but that they never desire anything else. (pp. 32–3)

Mill then went on to argue that while people do desire things 'which, in common language' are distinguished from happiness, they none the less always and only desire their own happiness. In spite of numerous attempts by Mill apologists to show that this argument is not as unsatisfactory as it seems, the most generally received view, that this proof contains blatant examples of two fallacies as well as a factual error, would seem to be correct. That Mill persisted with the argument even after criticism is not an adequate reason for supposing that this estimate rests on a misunderstanding of the argument. The proof commits the *fallacy of equivocation*, confusing 'desirable' meaning 'capable of being desired' with 'desirable' meaning 'worthy of being desired'. (It has been suggested that Mill did not use 'desirable' in the latter sense; if this is so, his fallacy would be that of *ignoratio elenchi*.) He noted that pleasure is desired, and concluded from this, via the word 'desirable', that pleasure is a worthy object of desire. The opening sentence, together with the analogies with 'visible' and 'audible', clearly reveal the character of Mill's argument. Apologists who argue that it is at least a first step to show that pleasure is capable of being desired (since only what can be desired can be desirable) do nothing to mitigate Mill's blunder, except thereby to construe it as being of a different kind. There is also *the fallacy of composition* which occurs when Mill argues that since each desires his own happiness, we all desire the happiness of all. We should desire the general happiness in desiring our own happiness only if our own happiness were the means to the general happiness. Even so, it would be misleading to express it this way. The seriousness of this fallacy is evident from the fact that this part of Mill's argument is his way of moving from egoistical hedonism (psychological egoism) to altruistic hedonism The attempt collapses at the outset. Mill himself, and some of his apologists, suggest that he really did not so argue, Mill in a letter writing:

> ... when I said that the general happiness is a good to the aggregate of all persons I did not mean that every human being's happiness is a good to every other human being though I think that in a good state of society and education it would be so. I merely meant in this particular sentence to argue that since A's happiness is a good, B's a good, C's a good, etc., the sum of all these goods must be a good.
>
> (13 June 1868, in *The Letters of John Stuart Mill*, ed. H. S. R. Elliot, II 116)

This is not what Mill had argued in *Utilitarianism*; and were it that, it would have needed to be reinforced by an argument showing that these goods are not such as in aggregate to enter into complexes or organic wholes which affect their value. In any case, the move suggested in the letter leaves a gap between what individual *A* desires and the general happiness. It is the greatest happiness that Mill sought to show to be the sole end; hence in terms of the premisses of his curious argument he must show that each person desires only the greatest happiness. Even the argument resting on the fallacy of composition fails to imply this. Further, as Mill came somewhat confusedly to acknowledge, we desire things other than pleasure – happiness, virtue, money. Mill wavered between acknowledging that we desire these as desirable for their own sakes, as parts of happiness, or as means to pleasure and for the pleasure we anticipate from them. The latter is the only position in consistency open to him, but for the reasons indicated by Butler and Hume it is untenable. We do not desire only pleasure for its own sake; nor do we desire only happiness for its own sake. Mill's move, that all we desire is either a means to or part of happiness, is equally untrue whether happiness is distinguished from or identified with pleasure. When we desire money, food, revenge, the welfare of our loved ones, we desire these things and not simply the pleasures or happiness the satisfaction of our desire may or may not bring. (See Bibliography for articles on Mill's proof.)

That Mill's defence of hedonistic utilitarianism is unsatisfactory does not mean that hedonistic utilitarianism is untenable. The more interesting defences since Mill are probably those of H. Sidgwick in *Methods of Ethics* in terms of intuitive insights into the two principles, of promotion of greatest pleasure and of its impartial distribution (stated as and claimed by Sidgwick to be one single principle), and J. J. C. Smart in *An Outline of Utilitarian Ethics* in terms of those pro-attitudes which commend themselves to benevolent men. These defences are also exposed to difficulties, the character of some of which can best be indicated by reference to Mill's introduction of an important new distinction into hedonistic utilitarianism, viz. that between higher and lower pleasures.

Higher and Lower Pleasures

As Mill noted, the utilitarian emphasis on maximising pleasure has provoked the persistent criticism that it involves enjoining the promoting of debased lives of sensual indulgence for ourselves and others; or as Aldous Huxley put it, by promoting *the brave new world*. If the greatest pleasure could in fact be achieved by catering for the sensual side of man, maximising the sensual satisfactions, then utilitarianism, as explained by Bentham and the Mills, would enjoin the organised rational self-indulgence of the maximum number in matters of food, drink, sex, as well as speed, excitement, etc., the self-indulgence stopping short of causing harm to self and others. Similarly, if more pleasure were to come from organised prostitution, legalised cruel sports and the like, the simple pleasure–pain utilitarianism would dictate that there be subsidised prostitution for the loveless, organised cruel sports for those whose pleasure is maximised in that way, and whose pleasures exceed the pain caused to the animals and animal-lovers. Further, as F. H. Bradley noted in *Ethical Studies*, such an ethic would make secret adultery which gave great pleasure to the adulterers and no pain to their spouses obligatory. Utilitarians have sought to deny that these conclusions follow by denying the factual claims in part or *in toto*. They commonly deny that greater pleasure comes from sensual indulgence and the so-called debased activities rather than from higher activities. They point to facts of the kinds noted by Bentham in terms of the intensity, duration, purity and fecundity of pleasures. None the less, as Bentham acknowledged in his celebrated statement concerning pushpin and poetry, there is no guarantee that these factual considerations will apply in all cases. Most of the claims made concerning intellectual pleasures in terms of their fecundity, comprehensiveness, etc., can be made as soundly concerning sensual pleasures – many men and women relive and re-enjoy in their thoughts a good meal, an affair, a conquest, a game – and the risks and pains that intellectual activities may involve are more to be avoided than even severe hangovers. Further, since many are incapable of entering into the higher pleasures, their contribution to the greatest pleasure, and our contribution in respect of them if we are unlike them, would often consist in their pursuing and being encouraged to pursue sensual pleasures. Hence the appeal to the facts of the pleasure–pain calculus leaves this version of utilitarianism open both in principle and in fact to the charge that it could and sometimes does enjoin sensuality as the highest form of existence to be promoted; the brave new world could well be the utilitarian's utopia.

Mill rejected such criticisms, first by suggesting that the pleasure–pain calculus, properly applied, did not lead to such conclusions, and then by adopting the radical course of distinguishing between higher and lower pleasures, between quality as well as quantity in respect of pleasure. He wrote here:

It is quite compatible with the principle of utility to recognise the fact, that some *kinds* of pleasure are more desirable and more valuable than others. It would be absurd that while, in estimating all other things, quality is considered as well as quantity, the estimation of pleasures should be supposed to depend on quantity alone.... It is better to be a human being dissatisfied than a pig satisfied; better to be Socrates dissatisfied than a fool satisfied. And if the fool, or the pig, are of a different opinion, it is because they only know their own side of the question. The other party to the comparison knows both sides. (*Utilitarianism*, pp. 7–9)

The only true or definite rule of conduct or standard of morality is the greatest happiness, but there is needed first a philosophical estimate of happiness. Quality as well as quantity of happiness is to be considered; less of a higher kind is preferable to more of a lower. The test of quality is the preference given by those who are acquainted with both. Socrates would rather choose to be Socrates dissatisfied than to be a pig satisfied. The pig *probably* would not, but then the pig knows only one side of the question; Socrates knows both.
(Diary 23 March 1854 [author's italics], in *Letters*, ed. Elliot)

On a question which is the best worth having of two pleasures, or which of two modes of existence is the most grateful to the feelings, apart from its moral attributes and from its consequences, the judgement of those who are qualified by knowledge of both, or, if they differ, that of the majority among them, must be admitted as final. And there needs be the less hesitation to accept this judgement respecting the quality of pleasures, since there is no other tribunal to be referred to even on the question of quantity. (p. 10)

Mill here was concerned to argue that a qualitatively superior pleasure, *ceteris paribus*, was more pleasurable than the qualitatively inferior pleasure, where the test of the pleasurableness of the pleasures is the preference of those who have experience of both types, i.e. the same test as that employed with quantities. The qualitative distinction Mill required here cannot be sustained. He sought to show that 2 units *qua* pleasure of a qualitatively superior pleasure are equal to 4, 6 or 8 units of a qualitatively inferior pleasure *qua* pleasure, but how could this be possible, if the units of pleasure mean anything at all? Alternatively, it may be argued that if all the qualitative distinctions which are reducible to quantitative ones – intensity, duration, purity, fecundity, etc. – are put aside, the remaining qualitative distinctions are not distinctive of quality *qua* pleasure, but *qua* value, where value must be interpreted in terms other than pleasure. Consider qualitative distinctions elsewhere. When we say that the Paris-model gown is qualitatively superior to the Woolworth's copy, that Danish cheese is superior to that of Australia, that wines of 1965 are superior to those of 1966, we are not asserting that the Paris gown, the Danish cheese, the wines of 1965 are in some sense quantitively greater than their inferior counterparts. We are saying, rather, that they are superior in respect of valued properties. It is with things such as fuel or petrol that the qualitative distinction seems to admit of reduction to quantity in the way Mill's argument about pleasure requires; Brand Z would be said, *ceteris paribus*, to be qualitatively superior to Brand X if it gives more miles to the gallon. However, that this judgement too involves reference to a standard of excellence distinct from quantity of petrol is clear from the fact that if Brand Z had unvalued properties, such as corroding the engine, it would be said, by reference to this same standard, to be an inferior petrol. Thus, as Mill's introductory sentences suggest, the reference to qualitatively higher pleasures as greater pleasures involves a departure from hedonistic utilitarianism towards ideal utilitarianism, i.e. acceptance of goods additional to

67

pleasure. (See G. E. Moore, *Principia Ethica*, p. 79, and F. H. Bradley, *Ethical Studies*, p. 120.)

Even had Mill been able to distinguish pleasures in the way he sought, without reference to a value judgement distinct from pleasure, he would not have succeeded in meeting the criticism in answer to which the distinction was introduced: for those who are incapable of enjoying the higher pleasures, the human 'pigs' and fools, utilitarianism would still dictate the promoting of their sensual pleasures (and, presumably, the pleasures of non-human animals) as part of the general happiness. The morally highest life for many people would remain the sensual life. Further, Mill argued for the superiority of the so-called higher pleasures as pleasures, from the preferences of those ordinary men (and the wise) who have experienced both types of pleasure. An examination of how ordinary and wise men judge suggests that they favour a life containing both types of pleasure, with somewhat greater stress laid on the so-called lower pleasures, with significant variation from individual to individual. However, few who who have successfully organised their lives for the maximum satisfaction of the lower pleasures express regret at having done so, whereas intellectuals, as C. P. Snow observed in *The New Men*, do commonly express doubts about the pleasure aspects of their styles of life. The truth is that different people find different things pleasant; some derive little pleasure from what others greatly enjoy. Some cannot enter fully into sensual enjoyments, others into intellectual pleasures. This suggests that the wise man, the intellectual man, are not necessarily competent judges; indeed, that the concept of a competent judge of the pleasures of all is one which has no application. All that can safely be said is that many intelligent men prefer one kind of pleasure, that many others prefer other kinds, and that most prefer a mixture of the two, the proportions varying from individual to individual. Mill sought to note such exceptions by suggesting that infirmity of character leads some to prefer the lower to the higher. Such an account of intelligent men of strong character choosing the lower pleasures of sex, food, drink, sport, excitement, when they could be enriching their intellectual lives and enjoying higher pleasures, as really being weak, is not true.

Mill's argument is that the pleasure which is preferred by those who have experience of both types of pleasure is necessarily more pleasurable. This would be true only if people, in their choices, were always motivated by a desire for pleasure, and hence that Socrates, in choosing the Socratic life, was moved to choose that life for the pleasure it brought him. This assumption is false. People choose modes of life, enter into activities, for many reasons, a common one being that they judge the mode of life or activity to be worth while in spite of their involving less pleasure than the alternatives. Mill, in this argument, as so often elsewhere, could not free himself from the false belief that our basic motivation is the thought of pleasure.

Thus Mill, in his own way, saw and acknowledged the value of certain kinds of activities and modes of life. His attempt to account for this value led him away from Benthamism towards an unclearly formulated and articulated ideal utilitarianism of the kind made explicit by G. E Moore, who so obviously owed much to Mill's *Utilitarianism*.

An interesting implication of a claim Mill made elsewhere in *Utilitarianism*, that duties to oneself are not strictly duties, is that in one's self-regarding behaviour one would commit no moral fault in pursuing the lower pleasures. The fault would be one of imprudence or aesthetics. Thus the distinction between higher and lower pleasures would not be as relevant and as effective as Mill suggested in securing utilitarianism from the criticism he noted; it would be compatible with a great deal of 'swinish' behaviour. This casts doubt on his claim that self-regarding duties are not duties; on any serious utilitarianism they must be such. Yet to concede this would involve drastic revision in Mill's accounts of obligation and the Art of Life.

After developing his proof, Mill sought to acknowledge that we appear to desire things other than pleasure and even happiness, by arguing that these are either means to or parts of happiness. He argued:

> The ingredients of happiness are very various, and each of them is desirable in itself, and not merely when considered as swelling an aggregate. The principle of utility does not mean that any given pleasure, as music, for instance, or any given exemption from pain, as for example health, is to be looked upon as means to a collective something termed happiness, and to be desired on that account. They are desired and desirable in and for themselves; besides being means, they are a part of the end. Virtue, according to the utilitarian doctrine, is not naturally and originally part of the end, but it is capable of becoming so; and in those who love it disinterestedly it has become so, and is desired and cherished, not as a means to happiness, but as a part of their happiness. (pp. 33–4)

Mill then argued that anything can come to be desired for its own sake, and, when so desired, it becomes a part of happiness. This means that happiness is the totality of things desired for themselves; and this includes virtue, and the virtues, and all things valued. It also means that what are the ingredients of happiness vary from person to person, from culture to culture. Mill concluded from this.

> Whatever is desired otherwise than as a means to some end beyond itself, and ultimately to happiness, is desired as itself a part of happiness, and is not desired for itself until it has become so. Those who desire virtue for its own sake, desire it either because the consciousness of it is a pleasure, or because the consciousness of being without it is a pain, or for both reasons united. (p. 35)

Desiring a thing and finding it pleasant, aversion to it and thinking of it as painful, are phenomena entirely inseparable, or rather two parts of the same phenomenon; in strictness of language, two different modes of naming the same psychological fact: that to think of an object as desirable (unless for the sake of its consequences), and to think of it as pleasant, are one and the same thing; and that to desire anything, except in proportion as the idea of it is pleasant, is a physical and metaphysical impossibility. (p. 36)

These are strange statements. The latter statement, as already noted, expresses a false view which permeates Mill's thinking in *Utilitarianism*; it explains in part Mill's reasons for some of the strange statements but ill accords with other claims. Mill asserted: (i) Happiness is the sum of things desirable in themselves, i.e. for Mill, desired for themselves. (ii) Music, money, virtue, may be desired for their own sakes and hence as part of happiness. (iii) Music, money, virtue, are desired for their own sakes only in so far as they are desired for the pleasure they give or are expected to give. (iv) Hence we always and only desire happiness. Mill's account of the relation between desire and pleasure is mistaken. Further, in any ordinary sense of 'desire for its own sake', to desire music, art or money for its own sake is to desire it independently of any anticipations in respect of pleasure or pain; thus (ii) and (iii) are contradictory if 'desire for its own sake' is interpreted in its ordinary sense. If it is not to be so interpreted, Mill would have failed to address himself to the real problem. Once Mill's confusion is eliminated, his argument lends itself to the view that pleasure and happiness are distinct, happiness being made up of what is desired for its own sake. This separation of pleasure and happiness opens the way to a variety of non-hedonistic utilitarian theories including extreme deontological theories, if and when the latter are held along the lines of honesty, etc., being desired for their own sakes. The account of happiness expressed in (i), when associated with the claim that almost anything may come to be desired for its own sake, means that for Mill almost anything at all may come to be an ingredient of happiness.

Had Mill simply claimed that happiness is the sole good, he would, in advancing his utilitarian ethic, have been advancing a very implausible, crude, naturalistic ethic, that the good is what is desired for its own sake. Besides being implausible, this is an unattractive theory at least in part because it is capable of morally unacceptable, anti-utilitarian conclusions. People can come to desire almost anything, hence they could come to desire the harm or suffering of animals, etc., and the ethic based on what is desired could involve the promoting of such evil. Unless happiness is more objective than this, the injunction 'Maximise happiness' has practical significance only when it is known what individuals desire for its own sake. Many of these desires will be relative to the individual, his society or culture. This means that a happiness calculus to guide our moral lives would be a practical impossibility to construct. The rules, judgements, conclusions of one age, generation or society would have little or no relevance for another. Mill sought to avoid this extreme relativity in terms of things being desired for themselves being desired for the pleasures we anticipate or obtain from them. Thus it was that he suggested that certain things are better desired for their own sakes than others, that people ought to be educated to desire these better things for their own sakes, for thereby greater overall pleasure will result. This retains pleasure, not happiness, as the sole good. In any case it is not a solution. Where there is no such ideal educational system in operation, people's uneducated desires would be the relevant ones. On the other hand, Mill's comments about moral education carry more than a suggestion of Platonic moral totalitarianism. It is relevant that Plato defended his educational programme in part as conducing to happiness.

Mill introduced various modifications which went some way towards lessening the clash between utilitarianism and conventional morality. Two such modifications have already been noted, the distinction between higher and lower pleasures, and the broadening of the concept of happiness, and the attempt thereby to accommodate within utilitarianism a love of virtue as an ingredient of happiness. Mill's treatment of the role of moral rules in utilitarian ethics fitted in with the same overall tendency, and while this may not have been his conscious intention, it was the effect of his various modifications.

Act Utilitarianism.

The principle of utility historically was construed as being both the test of which actions, rules, laws and institutions are morally desirable, and as the source of justification of all true moral judgements. In determining what course of action is obligatory, a utilitarian would ask himself 'Will this, of all possible actions, contribute most to the general happiness?' When considering whether to assent to a general rule of conduct, e.g. whether always to tell the truth, he will ask 'Would conformity with this rule lead to maximising happiness?' If the answer is 'No', he will reject the rule. If, on the whole, conformity with the rule is likely to lead to greater general happiness, he may use the rule as a useful rule of thumb and even encourage the stupid and thoughtless always to conform with the rule. Similarly with laws and conformity with the law. So, too, he will subject all political and social institutions, such as the political organisations, the institutions of private property and the family, to the test of utility. He will, of course, always seek to take full note of remote as well as more immediate effects. Such a utilitarian is an act utilitarian, the most famous act utilitarians apart from

73

Mill being Bentham, Sidgwick, Moore and Rashdall. All have stressed the complex issues and complexity of the calculations, but all, with the exception of Moore, believed the calculations to be practically possible. Many of Mill's remarks suggest that he, too, was an act utilitarian who accepted and used the greatest happiness principle in this way. Thus in the *Logic* he wrote:

> By a wise practitioner, therefore, rules of conduct will only be considered as provisional. Being made for the most numerous cases, or for those of most ordinary occurrence, they point out the manner in which it will be least perilous to act, where time or means do not exist for analysing the actual circumstances of the case, or where we cannot trust our judgement in estimating them. But they do not at all supersede the propriety of going through (when circumstances permit) the scientific process requisite for framing a rule from the data of the particular case before us. At the same time, the common rule may very properly serve as an admonition that a certain mode of action has been found by ourselves and others to be well adapted to the cases of most common occurrence; so that if it be unsuitable to the case in hand, the reason of its being so will be likely to arise from some unusual circumstance. (VI, 12, 3)

> How much greater still, then, must the error be of setting up such unbending principles, not merely as universal rules for attaining a given end, but as rules of conduct generally; without regard to the possibility, not only that some modifying cause may prevent the attainment of the given end by the means which the rule prescribes, but that success itself may conflict with some other end, which may possibly chance to be more desirable. (VI, 12, 4)

These remarks relate to the Art of Life of which morality is a part. So too, in the essay *Dr Whewell on Moral Philosophy*, Mill's contemptuous dismissal of Paley as one who deduced from utilitarian premises all the orthodox conclusions suggests that it is act utilitarianism which he takes seriously. The reply to Whewell's criticism of utilitarianism concerning the difficulty of calculating the consequences, drawing as it does an analogy with prudence, confirms the act utilitarian interpretation. An act utilitarian view is also expressed in *Bentham*, although there it is a more explicitly cautious, moderate version, and one easily confused with a very different form of utilitarianism, rule utilitarianism, that rules are tested (justified) by reference to the greatest happiness principle, and acts by reference to the rules. Mill in one place suggests that the principle of utility should be viewed as an *explanatory* premiss, rather than as a test to which we directly appeal to determine our duty. The practical life is said to be too complex to allow the direct appeal. Thus this suggestion that we do not appeal to utility directly is not a theoretical restriction as in rule utilitarianism but one urged because of the complexities of the situations. In the revised version of the essay in *Dissertations and Discussions*, Mill explicitly allowed an appeal to the principle of utility when the secondary principles collide (see *Dissertations and Discussions*, pp. 384–5). The dominant view in *Utilitarianism* is an act utilitarianism which falls between the radical Benthamite one and the cautious conservative approach of the essay *Bentham*, although Mill did at times suggest a rule utilitarian view, without seeming to notice the difference between it and act utilitarianism, and even though his account of justice is basically a rule utilitarian account. Evidence in support of the act utilitarian interpretation includes first the statement: 'When we engage in a pursuit, a clear and precise conception of what we are pursuing would seem to be the first thing we need, instead of the last we are to look forward to. A test of right and wrong must be the means, one would think, of ascertaining what is right or wrong, and not a consequence of having already ascertained it' (p. 2). A contrast with science is drawn. Secondly, Mill noted the value of feelings concerning veracity but still allowed that the rule admits of excep-

75

tions. 'But in order that the exception may not extend itself beyond the need, and may have the least possible effect in weakening reliance on veracity, it ought to be recognised, and, if possible, its limits defined; and if the principle of utility is good for anything, it must be good for weighing these conflicting utilities against one another, and marking out the region within which one or the other preponderates' (p. 21). The next paragraph takes up the objection that there is not time before an action to weigh the effects of alternative possible actions. Mill did not reply by rejecting such calculations as irrelevant but by suggesting that the calculation is crucial but has already been made, and the answer embodied in the moral rules of society:

> The answer to the objection is, that there has been ample time, namely, the whole past duration of the human species. During all that time, mankind have been learning by experience the tendencies of actions; on which experience all the prudence, as well as all the morality of life, are dependent. ... It is truly a whimsical supposition that, if mankind were agreed in considering utility to be the test of morality, they would remain without any agreement as to what *is* useful, and would take no measures for having their notions on the subject taught to the young, and enforced by law and opinion. (p. 22)

Mill then went on to speak of moral rules as corollaries and as 'intermediate generalisations' from the principle of utility, observing:

> It is a strange notion that the acknowledgment of a first principle is inconsistent with the admission of secondary ones. To inform a traveller respecting the place of his ultimate destination, is not to forbid the use of landmarks and direction-posts on the way. The proposition that happiness is the end and aim of morality, does not mean that no road ought to be laid down to that goal, or that persons going thither should not be advised to take one direction rather

76

than another. ... Nobody argues that the art of navigation is not founded on astronomy, because sailors cannot wait to calculate the Nautical Almanack. Being rational creatures, they go to sea with it ready calculated; and all rational creatures go out upon the sea of life with their minds made up on the common questions of right and wrong, as well as on many of the far more difficult questions of wise and foolish. ... *Whatever we adopt as the fundamental principle of morality, we require subordinate principles to apply it by; the impossibility of doing without them, being common to all systems, can afford no argument against any one in particular.* (pp. 22–3; author's italics)

Here Mill was not enjoining blind conformity with the rules, but that we use rules based on calculated predictions of consequences in the way we use other practical rules. Where we find an evident miscalculation, or that special circumstances prevail, we rely on our own calculations. At the foot of p. 23 Mill noted that the moral agent has discretion to judge the right action on the basis of the peculiar circumstances of the case.

Benthamite utilitarianism involves the conclusion that whenever the consequences of an action are such that it brings greater happiness than any other action, that action is right whether it be an act of injustice, betrayal, cruelty, false witness, lying, cheating or the like. Mill's cautious practical approach, with his suggestion that the normal thing is to conform with the moral rules of society, except where there are good reasons for believing that by so acting we will not promote the general happiness, or except where these rules conflict, reduces the range of cases in which utilitarianism will be seen to involve flying in the face of conventional morality. However, if the moral rules are rationally and thoughtfully appraised, many more exceptions would seem to be dictated than Mill suggested. Like so many other utilitarians, Mill wrote as if the moral rules of society were summaries, not of the moral wisdom of the ages as Burke would have argued,

77

but of the hedonistic utilitarian wisdom of the ages. He likened the moral rules of his day in *Utilitarianism*, but not in his letters, to the moral almanac calculated on the basis of the truth of utilitarianism, as if men of past ages had consciously or unconsciously sought to devise rules which best promoted the general pleasure. This is unhistorical nonsense, or at best simply wishful thinking. Moral rules have come into being from superstitious, religious and anti-utilitarian sources; they have often been based on false beliefs, and yet have continued to be accepted long after the beliefs on which they were based have been rejected, and in spite of utilitarian attempts to modify or reject them. Mill was aware of this concerning marriage.

That rules tend to 'lag behind' the utilitarian wisdom of a society is shown by the fact that hedonistic utilitarians battle, often with much delay and little success, to change the moral rules of their societies. Clearly, with changing, increasing knowledge, with greater control over our environment and our lives, what is the best way of promoting the general pleasure is likely to change. Here the increased knowledge concerning homosexuality, free love, the increased control over the consequences of actions provided by birth control, abortion and control of V.D. is relevant.

There are good grounds for believing that such basic rules as those of veracity, fidelity, justice are *usually* conducive to the greatest good; it is less clear that they are as conducive to the greatest happiness. Mill's attempt to render utilitarianism less radical and a more cautious, conservative, explanatory theory is not successful. Without further detailed argument by Mill, it must be accepted that his utilitarianism would lead to serious conflicts with commonsense morality in a way damaging to utilitarian ethics. Awareness of this general difficulty has led many utilitarians during the past two decades to revive and develop the version now known as rule utilitarianism.

This is not a single theory but a variety of theories. The core theory of which the others are varieties may be stated: 'An action is justified or seen to be right by showing that it is in accord with a moral rule, where the rule is such that the recognition of it (or practice in accord with it) promotes the greatest happiness or good.' Even this may be too equivocal a statement of the theory, as an act utilitarian, with appropriate calculations, could accept such an ethic. The rule utilitarian insists that departures from the rule, where the rule is a useful one, or the most useful available or possible one, are wrong. Rule utilitarianism can be qualified in various ways, with conditions written into the rule, but the more conditions admitting of exceptions on utilitarian grounds that are written into the rule, the nearer the theory comes to coinciding with act utilitarianism. In various places Mill seems to hold or to entertain a rule utilitarian theory. Thus in the *Logic* in the passage immediately following the statement 'I do not mean to assert that the promotion of happiness should be the end of all actions, or even of all rules of action', Mill could perhaps be interpreted as advancing a rule utilitarian theory, although a careful reading would suggest that he is making a point about tactics for act utilitarians to adopt. That in *Utilitarianism* and *Bentham* Mill sometimes suggested that utility is to be appealed to only when there are conflicts between the rules, has been construed as evidence of a rule utilitarian theory by J. O. Urmson ('The Interpretation of the Moral Philosophy of J. S. Mill', *Philosophical Quarterly*, III (1953) 33–9). However, the passage in *Utilitarianism* following that which impressed Urmson undercuts its value, for it runs: 'There is no case of moral obligation in which some secondary principle is not involved; and if only one, there can seldom be any real doubt which one it is, in the mind of any person by whom the principle itself is recognised' (p. 24). The use of the word 'seldom' here opens the way for the possibility of a direct appeal to utility when in doubt about the rule. Although he rejects Urmson's interpretation, J. D. Mabbott notes that some of Mill's statements do suggest such an interpretation, for example the passage beginning at the foot of p. 17 where Mill suggests that we should abstain from a beneficial act if it is of a kind which is generally harmful. This, like Mill's concern to educate and use moral feelings to promote the practice of utilitarianism, does harmonise with rule utilitarianism, but it is equally intelligible on act utilitarianism. Many writers attach significance to Mill's use of the words 'tends' and 'tendency', since they relate to classes and not to individual acts. In fact Mill took the words over from Bentham and used them very carelessly. Thus although, as noted above, Mill's account of justice is a rule utilitarian one, his dominant position was that of an act utilitarian.

A number of considerations has influenced many utilitarians to abandon act in favour of rule utilitarianism. One is that indicated in the *Logic*, that greater utility overall is likely to be achieved by general conformity with useful rules, even though occasional, well-judged departures from them might increase the general happiness. Mill's point was not that it is impossible to achieve both the small and the big gains which come from cultivating respect for the rule; rather it is a point about tactics. We are more likely to achieve the larger, long-term, widespread gains if we forgo the immediate gains by breaking the rule. This looks like a sophisticated version of act utilitarianism and would be such if the suggestion were that the probabilities of maximising happiness by making exceptions to the rule, or by enjoying conformity with it, be weighed, and deciding that the balance of probabilities lay with the latter. This is not the rule utilitarian's position. His position is that we may *know* that we achieve less pleasure (or good) by refraining from ignoble acts. The act utilitarian seeks to achieve both. The rule utilitarian is prepared knowingly to sacrifice some lesser pleasures (goods), his apparent justification being in terms of more certain, greater happiness (good). The less the risk of failure which is involved in striving for both, the more rule utilitarianism involves an abandonment of an ethic of consequences.

The other drive to rule utilitarianism, especially during the past twenty years, has come from the hope that it will provide a solution to the utilitarian's problem of showing that utilitarianism is not the harsh, shocking, inhumane theory it appeared to be in Bentham's hands, and which even a sympathetic interpretation of it seems to expose it as being. It enjoins injustices wherever greater happiness comes from injustice. Consider examples of useful, unjust punishment: punishment of innocent men who are believed to be guilty, as deterrents against crime; of those not responsible for their actions, e.g. many deserters in wartime; excessive punishment as a deterrent; collective punishment; and the like. As Sidgwick acknowledged, it may make hypocrisy a virtue, even concerning one's acceptance of the principle of utility itself; it renders the duties of fidelity and veracity subject to serious qualification; and, as F. H. Bradley noted in *Ethical Studies*, it may enjoin secret adultery as a virtue, e.g. when associated with a hypocritical, expressed approval of the sanctity of marriage, where the adulterers take the greatest care that they harm no others, etc. Many, although not all, utilitarians are uneasy about such implications of act utilitarianism. Many deny that they hold, appealing to factual considerations to maintain that greater general happiness (or good) will not result from such acts, that less obvious, more indirect consequences such as the effects on the characters and moral habits of the parties involved, the general respect for useful rules and institutions, are such as to outweigh any good that may come from such acts. However, it is easy to point to actual cases where these considerations do not apply, where the moral judgement about the wrongness of the act remains evidently true. It is also easy to construct possible situations parallel to situations which do occur, to confirm that act utilitarianism may and does have such implications. Hence some utilitarians look to rule utilitarianism as a way of retaining what they see as the essential inspiration of utilitarianism while avoiding these implications.

There are many grounds for rejecting rule utilitarianism. As J. J. C. Smart has convincingly argued, it involves an abandonment of utilitarianism for pointless rule-worship. Consider the example: A weak person, under the influence of drink, is inveigled by skilful but technically honest card players into gambling beyond his means. He signs an I.O.U. for £10,000 and promises, when sober, to repay this amount by instalments. The next day his daughter is severely burned on the face, requiring expensive plastic surgery to avoid permanent, gross disfigurement. If his appeals to his creditors fail, the act utilitarian would reasonably consider breaking his agreement and buying the plastic surgery. The rule utilitarian, however, would say, 'No, to do that would be to break a promise (or contract) and infringe socially useful rules; the test of right and wrong is the rule.' This is blind, morally objectionable rule-worship. It is also very different from a Kantian or Rossian position where the reason offered for conforming with the rule is that actions based on principles have a worth of their own. The rule utilitarian does not say that; he urges conformity because the rule is a useful rule, yet he demands conformity even when this causes avoidable unhappiness. In the above example, he might seek an escape by writing this sort of exception into the rule. There are difficulties here – such exceptions as are morally necessary are not always socially recognised as such; – yet to allow the moral agent the right to determine which exceptions he may legitimately write into his rules is to defeat the intention of the rule. This links with a more general difficulty.

Which rules are the relevant rules for the rule utilitarian? A variety of answers is open to him. The more obvious alternatives are: (*a*) the rules actually recognised and acted upon in one's society; (*b*) those rules of one's society which are useful or more useful than other possible rules; (c) those rules (principles) which are not currently recognised but which would be useful if adopted as social rules. Mill, in so far as he entertained rule utilitarianism, and many rule utilitarians opt for conformity with the rules actually recognised in one's society; the talk about such rules as summaries of utilitarian wisdom suggests this view. It encounters obvious difficulties. In a society in which slaves are personal property, covered by property rules condemning theft, to seek illegally to emancipate a slave of another, even though it caused little inconvenience to the owner and great happiness to the slave, would be wrong. In a society in which only monogamous, indissoluble marriage was morally accepted, to cohabit with one's lover because one did not wish to make her legally one's chattel (as to an extent a wife became in Mill's day) would be gravely wrong even though no one was harmed thereby and both parties were made happy. In a society in which homosexuality was condemned, for two homosexuals to set up house together would be immoral even though they became happier, better-adjusted individuals. Further, if one is obliged to conform with such rules, it is hard to see how it can be right at the same time to seek to change them by undermining them and weakening public respect for them, as a utilitarian ought, if more useful social rules are possible.

If the relevant rules are those which are useful or more useful than other possible social rules, most of these points would still hold. Most property rules, even those rendering slaves private property, are useful rules, and almost any rules governing sexual behaviour are better than no rules. On the other hand, if the rules that are to be obeyed are the most useful available rules, we should have to assess the relevant rules with different people reaching different conclusions. In that case, by acting on their judgements, they will undermine public confidence in the observance of the rules, and hence the utility thereof. As it is unlikely that any one single existing rule is the best practicable rule, a considerable indeterminacy could enter here.

Both positions (*a*) and (*b*) have the common defect of being versions of relativism. The cannibal, the Greek infanticidist, the Spartan, the slave-master may be equally good men on such a utilitarian relativism. In fact it is often right to act contrary to the rules of one's society, and one of Bentham's great contributions, and that of many utilitarians since, has been to stress this fact, and hence the need for constant review and reform of defective social and legal rules.

The suggestion that we should act, not on the basis of actually recognised rules, but in conformity with rules which would be useful if they were to become socially adopted, is an even stranger one; it is the view of rule utilitarianism suggested by R. M. Hare in *Freedom and Reason*, and it would imply that the right action is that based upon a principle which would be useful if generally adopted, whether or not it has been or is likely to be generally adopted, and irrespective of the nature of the consequences. What is true and important in utilitarianism is that the consequences of our actions are relevant to their morality. What is mistaken is the claim that they are the only relevant consideration. The character of an act as one of lying, cheating, betraying, is also relevant. What is mistaken in this version of rule utilitarianism, a version Mill gave no hint of adopting, is that it invites us to disregard completely the actual consequences and to concentrate entirely on the possible, albeit unlikely, consequences which would follow if anyone acted on the basis of the rule or principle on which we base our action.

Duty and Obligation

Mill equated 'right', 'obligatory' and 'duty' in chap. 5 of *Utilitarianism* and, in a curious discussion, sought to develop an account of obligation distinct from that in terms of Utility, and in such a way that it is unclear whether what he advanced was intended to be an analytic, synthetic *a priori*, or merely contingent statement

84

about right and obligatory actions. Mill sought to relate being under an obligation with the notions 'ought to be punished', 'deserving of punishment':

> We do not call anything wrong, unless we mean to imply that a person ought to be punished in some way or other for doing it; if not by law, by the opinion of his fellow-creatures; if not by opinion, by the reproaches of his own conscience.... It is a part of the notion of Duty in every one of its forms, that a person may rightfully be compelled to fulfil it. Duty is a thing which may be *exacted* from a person, as one exacts a debt. Unless we think that it may be exacted from him, we do not call it his duty. Reasons of prudence, or the interest of other people, may militate against exacting it; but the person himself, it is clearly understood, would not be entitled to complain. There are other things, on the contrary, which we wish that people should do, which we like and admire them for doing, perhaps dislike or despise them for not doing, but yet admit that they are not bound to do; it is not a case of moral obligation; we do not blame them, that is, we do not think that they are proper objects of punishment. (p. 45)

This is the account of moral obligation set out in A. Bain's *The Emotions and the Will*, chap. xv, to which Mill referred his reader. Bain observed of the words 'Morality, Duty, Obligation, or Right' that 'the proper meaning, or import, of these terms refers to that class of action which is enforced by the sanction of punishment'. He then went on to note three powers in the sphere of punishment: Law, Society and Conscience (pp. 286–7). Although Mill appears here to follow Bain in equating 'right', 'ought' and 'duty', the words in their ordinary usage are significantly different, 'ought' and 'duty' suggesting constraint in a way 'right' does not. Even as an account of obligation it will not do. There is neither an analytic, nor a universal, contingent connection between an action being obligatory and the idea that the person who fails to perform it

85

ought or deserves to be punished. Mill weakened the notion of punishment so that even twinges of conscience came for him to count as such, but while we may believe it to be appropriate and even desirable that those who fail to do what they ought should feel pangs of conscience, this is not what we mean to assert when we claim that X was obligatory on A, nor are we guilty of any great paradox if we assert of one who has not done what he ought, that it is a good thing he is not feeling remorse. Thus a Roman Catholic may say to a doctor who has performed an abortion 'You morally ought not to have performed that operation' without implying or believing that the doctor ought or deserves to be punished by the state, society or his conscience. Mill's account is further unsatisfactory because it makes use of a concept, or concepts, as obscure as that it is seeking to explain, explaining obligation in terms of 'ought' and/or desert, or merit, where the 'ought' is a moral ought, and desert and merit concepts of justice. Mill sought to explain justice by reference to obligations and rights, yet here we find that obligation, if not explained circularly, is to be explained in terms of concepts of justice. Hence justice would be explained circularly. (The discussion of responsibility in *Hamilton* suggests that merit and desert here would ultimately be explained in terms of 'useful to punish because responsive to punishment'.) The discussion also introduces the concept 'entitled', a concept closely linked with that of a right. Rights are explained by Mill in terms of obligations, obligations themselves in terms of 'ought', desert, merit and 'entitled'. In so doing, Mill appears to have moved away from the naturalistic utilitarianism of Bentham; in fact, he sought to explain these concepts too in utilitarian terms, albeit, it will be argued, unsuccessfully.

This whole account of duty as 'a thing which may be exacted ... as one exacts a debt', has an unpleasantly illiberal flavour. This is especially so if the greatest happiness principle is interpreted as it is by most utilitarians, although not by Mill himself in his aside about duties to oneself not being duties, as counting the agent's happiness as part of the general happiness and thereby creating duties. These would, on this view, be duties which may be exacted, which the agent may be compelled to fulfil. Mill did not take this view about self-regarding duties, nor did he specify whether it was of all types or only some that the coerced person was not entitled to complain when made to do his duty.

Mill nowhere explained his grounds for denying self-regarding duties to be duties, and one is forced to conclude that his premiss is that of the essay on *Liberty*, conjoined with this analysis of obligation, in which case this analysis has importance as qualifying his acceptance of utilitarianism. We find, instead of a defence of his claim concerning self-regarding duties, elaborations of it which reveal the extent of his qualification of utilitarian ethics. In the *Logic*, *Bentham* and *Utilitarianism* Mill noted that there are other ways of judging actions besides in terms of their morality. In the *Logic* he distinguished *three departments* in the Art of Life, viz. Morality, Prudence or Policy and Aesthetics (vi, 12, 6); in *Bentham* he distinguished different *aspects of actions*, the moral, the aesthetic and the sympathetic (lovable) aspect; in *Utilitarianism* he distinguished morality, expediency and worthiness. His view appears to have been that some actions have all aspects, moral, aesthetic, prudence, but that others fall only into one or two of the departments of life.

Utility and Justice

Clashes between the claims of justice and utility, for example in respect of useful but unjust deterrent punishment, create what many utilitarians see to be a source of major difficulties for utilitarianism. Here it is often argued that many of the alleged clashes between justice and utility are only apparent and not real, and that where there are real clashes, the morally right course to follow is that dictated by utility. This was, in effect, Mill's approach in his obscure and tortuous discussion in chap. 5 of *Utilitarianism*. This discussion was originally intended as a separate essay, hence its argument is not tightly integrated with the remainder of *Utilitarianism*.

Mill sought to explain the strength of our feeling concerning justice by contrast with other duties, to mark off from other duties the duties of justice, and at the same time to explain the claims of justice in utilitarian terms. He offered a number of accounts, but the dominant one is that justice relates to duties to determinate persons, which those persons have the right to exact, and where an injustice involves a breach of a right. A right is explained in terms of four things: (i) A rule relating to essentials of well-being, the breach of which involves hurt to assignable persons. (ii) A demand for punishment, Mill tracing this demand back to a desire for revenge, plus sympathy for others. (iii) A claim on the state or society to protect the individual harmed by the breach of the rule. (iv) The claim to protection is grounded on utility, the claims of utility here being greater than those created by duties not called duties of justice. Mill qualified this latter claim to note that there may be exceptions where utility dictates the overriding of the claims of justice for the sake of other duties or rules.

Each aspect of this account may be questioned. Injustices may result not only from breaches of rules, but from strict enforcement of socially useful, even generally just rules. Injustices need not involve anything which may be described in such strong terms as 'a hurt to the injured person'; a man may be treated unjustly by being passed over for an honour he neither covets nor desires. While we usually feel strongly about injustices, and are glad to see unjust persons suffer for their injustice, it is not true that we always demand punishment for an injustice; consider here unjust parental treatment, or the injustice of an employer in appointing a less talented but more beautiful woman as his secretary at a time when jobs are hard to come by. The rights involved in injustices need not be socially important; certainly, they need not be of overriding importance. Consider rewards for labour; what is dictated

88

by utility as useful social rules here may be very different from what is seen to be just; the rules seen to be just come to be important socially for this very reason. It would be hard today to sustain Mill's claim that the factors relevant to justice here are those relevant to social utility. So, too, it is exposed to all the objections to which rule utilitarian accounts of punishment are exposed, namely that systems of punishment which involve punishment of innocent persons (under retroactive laws, collective and scapegoat punishment), of persons not responsible for their actions but who are generally believed to be responsible and the like, may be dictated by rules of social utility conferring rights, and yet be gravely unjust. Similarly, the rules relating to the inequality of women, to which Mill took such strong objection as being unjust, were defended as vital to the social well-being. Whether the rights accorded slave-masters, for example, in ancient Greece were dictates of justice, would on Mill's account be determined by reference to the social utility of the rights and the rules on which they were based. It has been argued by many, including utilitarians, that such rights have a justification in terms of social utility in situations such as found in ancient Greece. Thus an action may be unjust by commonsense standards and just by Mill's standards, and vice versa. To the extent that this is so, Mill's account fails to explain the character of the specific duties of justice, and to deal with the problems that arise concerning this duty for utilitarianism.

Further, Mill explicitly allowed that the claims of justice, as he explained justice, may on occasion be overridden by considerations of utility. He gave no clear guidance concerning when, and why; hence whether these exceptions create difficulties for utilitarianism depends entirely on how these unjust acts are determined. This links with the general character of Mill's claim as an empirical claim. He argues that the recognition of some rules, duties and rights is socially of great importance, and for this reason to be called duties of justice. Yet there is a complete absence of any attempt to offer any empirical considerations. Most notably, there is no attempt to consider such unjust institutions and practices as deterrent punishment, where punishment is in excess of what is deserved, of a collective kind, etc., nor is there any attempt to show that the rights infringed by such practices are such that it is socially of vital importance that they be respected. This he could not do, because his account of moral responsibility committed him to a defence of such unjust punishment.

Freedom, Responsibility and Punishment

Mill explained the libertarian view as maintaining 'that the will is not determined, like other phenomena, by antecedents, but determines itself; that our volitions are not, properly speaking, the effects of causes, or at least have no causes which they uniformly and implicitly obey' (*Logic*, VI, 2, 1). Because he construed motives and reasons as causes, he thereby interpreted the libertarian view in a way F. H. Bradley later expressed as his own, namely that a free self is a capricious, random self. Mill rejected this view, not as Bradley later did, on the basis of its incompatibility with the 'vulgar view of responsibility', but by questioning the considerations on which it is based and adducing positive considerations for the necessitarian view. Mill rejected the argument from introspection on the proper ground that consciousness cannot reveal whether or not we are caused, but only what we feel; hence he also rejected the kinds of examples cited in this century by C. A. Campbell of overcoming moral temptation as not showing that we can act in opposition to our strongest desires (see C. A. Campbell, *Selfhood and Godhood*, lecture IX). In support of the determinist view, Mill relied on an appeal to universal causation, arguing thus:

Correctly conceived, the doctrine called Philosophical Necessity is simply this: that, given the motives which are present to an individual's mind, and given likewise the character and disposition of the individual, the manner in which he will act may be unerringly inferred: that if we knew the person thoroughly, and knew all the inducements which are acting upon him, we could foretell his conduct with as much certainty as we can predict any physical event. This proposition I take to be a mere interpretation of universal experience, a statement in words of what everyone is internally convinced of. (*Logic*, VI, 2, 2)

They [the Necessitarians] affirm, as a truth of experience, that volitions do, in point of fact, follow determinate moral antecedents with the same uniformity, and [when we have sufficient knowledge of the circumstances] with the same certainty, as physical effects follow their physical causes. These moral antecedents are desires, aversions, habits and dispositions, combined with outward circumstances suited to call those internal incentives into action. All these again are effects of causes, those of them which are mental being consequences of education, and of other moral and physical influences. This is what Necessitarians affirm: and they court every possible mode in which its truth can be verified. (*Hamilton*, 5th ed., pp. 576–7; all subsequent references are to this edition)

This is supported by the surprisingly confident claim that experience has established that our actions are subject to causality in Mill's sense of causality, i.e. invariable sequence. The libertarian in fact does not operate with this notion of cause when asserting freedom of the will. It is of note that Mill did not argue, as have many recent philosophers, that universal causality holds, but that what we mean by free choice or action, e.g. freely choosing one's bride, is not necessarily incompatible with there being universal causation. However, he did develop a strange argument which has affinities with this, suggesting that we have a limited freedom in that we are capable of making or changing our characters if we so choose (*Hamilton*, pp. 601–2). This left Mill with a problem concerning moral responsibility. The ordinary man's view is that unless an action is freely chosen, he is not responsible for it; that responsibility involves freedom, such that if there is no free will there is no moral responsibility, and no such thing as morality. Mill saw and faced his problem, asking what we mean by moral responsibility and answering 'responsibility means punishment', and then explaining this statement in terms of a feeling of liability to punishment, and this in turn in terms of either an expectation that we shall be punished, or a feeling that we deserve punishment (*Hamilton*, pp. 586–7). As an autobiographical statement this is interesting and throws light on James Mill's educative methods. As a statement about responsibility it is seriously astray. Owning or acknowledging the action as our own is what is central to the idea of responsibility. If we are reared in a reward-conscious environment, we may closely associate responsibility and the thought of rewards and being deserving of rewards; if brought up in a punishment environment we may think of punishment and of being deserving of punishment. The crucial idea, however, is that the act is ours, that we own it. No doubt there is a factual connection between an act being ours and our being liable to punishment for it if it fails to measure up to the punisher's standards, but this is a contingent, non-universal connection, not a conceptual one.

Mill argued thus because he was concerned to retain the notion of desert by explaining human conduct as controllable by fear of punishment, and actions deserving of punishment as those which would have been prevented by the thought of the punishment. Thus, for Mill, the person deserving of punishment is not necessarily he who acts very badly, but rather the person who, if intimidated by fear of punishment, would not have acted badly. Hence to say 'The punishment was deserved' would, for Mill, amount to saying 'It was punishment calculated to deter him from the evil action'. Mill summed up his position, observing that 'Punishment proceeds on the assumption that the will is governed by motives. If punishment had no power of acting on the will, it would be illegitimate, however natural might be the inclination to inflict it' (*Hamilton*, p. 592). Mill then proceeded to argue that punishment is justified when it is for the benefit of the offender, and when involved in protecting the rights of others. The former claim is associated with the surprising contention that the normal condition of man is that of loving right (as understood by utilitarians presumably), and that the punishment, or fear of it, restores the evil man to the normal condition. Punishment to protect rights is said to be just because and in so far as the rights are just, i.e. real rights. Since, in *Utilitarianism*, Mill had explained rights as grounded on duties in others, punishment is just when it protects those to whom duties are owed. Sharply in contrast with the spirit of the essay *Liberty*, Mill here argued:

To punish him [the offender] for his own good, provided the inflictor has any proper title to constitute himself a judge, is no more unjust than to administer medicine. As far, indeed as respects the criminal himself, the theory of punishment is that, by counterbalancing the influence of present temptations, or acquired bad habits, it restores the mind to that normal preponderance of the love of right, which many moralists and theologians consider to constitute the true definition of our freedom. In its other aspect, punishment is a precaution taken by society in self-defence. To make this just, the only condition required is, that the end which society is attempting to enforce by punishment, should be a just one. Used as a means of aggression by society on the just rights of the individual, punishment is unjust. Used to protect the just rights of others against unjust aggression by the offender, it is just. If it is possible to have just rights ... it cannot be unjust to defend them. Free-will or no free-will, it is just to punish so far as is necessary for this purpose, as it is just to put

93

a wild beast to death (without unnecessary suffering)
for the same object. (*Hamilton*, pp 592–4)

That capacity to react to fear of punishment is something distinct from responsibility is clear from two
facts: (i) that animals and compulsives may be conditioned to react to fear of punishment and yet remain
not responsible for their actions in any morally relevant sense; and (ii) that many human beings, e.g. so-
called incorrigible criminals, are relatively or completely unmoved by fear and yet may be free agents
responsible for their actions. That punishment does
not become just by being for the good of the offender
or for the protection of the rights of others is also clear.
A person may have a minor but deeply ingrained
moral flaw in his character; for example, he may be a
near-compulsive liar, and everyone know this, and he
do little harm. Punishment to correct this flaw may
involve years of savage treatment. Such punishment
would be unjust, unjust because disproportionate.
Similarly with offences against the rights of others. The
punishment necessary for effective deterrence may be
quite disproportionate to the seriousness of the offence.
Kleptomaniacs, alcoholics, persistent violators of road
laws can probably be deterred if the punishment is
made severe and certain enough. Daily torture, public
humiliation, and fear of such may produce the desired
result; but such punishment would be unjust, excessive
and undeserved. Justice in punishment is one thing;
success in reforming the criminal or in deterring others
are quite distinct.

A fundamental objection to Mill's account of justice
in punishment is that it presupposes that there are
people who are subject to real obligations. Mill likened
the offender to the beast of prey which is killed. His
account of offences against others involves a very
different view of human beings, namely, that they are
bearers of real obligations. Here it might well be
asked: Can a being who is necessitated to act as he does,
or, in Mill's language, is caused to act as he does, be a
bearer of duties? Can he be obliged to act in a way

other than that in which he is causally determined to act (or in which he prefers to act)? Can he justly be punished for doing what he does, when 'he' is a mere collection or temporary meeting place of causes? The fact that fear of punishment may affect the result is completely irrelevant to the issues of whether he is subject to obligations, and whether he is justly punished for invading the rights of another. If he and all human beings are necessitated to do what they do, there are no possessors of rights, and no question of justice.

A utilitarian who is also a determinist is forced to construe punishment, praise and blame, ascription of responsibility, and the like, as manipulative devices, on a parallel with punishment of animals and young children. In doing this he deprives himself of any legitimate ground for construing any punishment as just or unjust. However, by adopting this very view, he in the very act renounces it. The notion of manipulation is that of acting, causing, freely changing another. Thus to adopt the view of punishment as manipulation is itself to adopt, while rejecting, the libertarian view. It is of course possible to give a longer story according to which manipulation is not real manipulation, but itself a product of prior causes; but if such an account were to be filled in, the point of talk of justice, responsibility and punishment would become less evident.

In bulk and importance Mill's political writings are the most substantial of his contributions to philosophy. The more important include: *Principles of Political Economy* (1848, with many later editions), especially bk II, chaps 1, 2, 5, 11–13; bk IV, chap. 7; bk V, chaps 1, 2, 10, 11; *On Liberty* (1859); *Considerations on Representative Government* (1861); *The Subjection of Women* (1869). Also of importance are: *The Spirit of the Age* (1831), *The Rationale of Political Representation* (1835), *Tocqueville on Democracy in America* (1835, 1840), *Civilization* (1836), *Bentham* (1838), *Reorganization of the Reform Party* (1839), *Coleridge* (1840), *Essays on Some Unsettled Questions of Political Economy* (1844), *The Claims of Labour* (1845), *Recent Writers on Reform* (1859), *Thoughts on Parliamentary Reform* (1859), *Auguste Comte and Positivism* (1865), and the posthumous *Chapters on Socialism* (1879). In addition, much of the *Autobiography* and of bk VI of the *Logic* is relevant. Many more of Mill's essays of nearly equal importance could well have been mentioned here.

As a political philosopher Mill is best known today as the author of *Liberty*, as the Apostle of Liberty, the person who has set out the clearest, most unequivocal, best-argued defence to date of individual liberty. Yet *Liberty* is the least typical, although probably the most important, of Mill's political essays. It is untypical because in it he sought to defend a single truth as if it were subject to no substantial qualification; he was pro-*laissez-faire*, unqualifiedly individualistic, and completely egalitarian; he appeared unconcerned about historical development (although he restricted his claims concerning liberty to civilised, mature persons);

and he was hostile to tradition and customs, stressing the danger of tyranny of custom, and the evils thereof. By contrast, in his other writings Mill usually pressed views in highly qualified ways. This is most evidently so in his discussions of liberty (outside of *Liberty*), democracy and socialism. He was not consistently libertarian, individualistic and egalitarian. Rather, Mill was given to enthusiasms for ideas and for people, and for a time at least was much influenced by Coleridge and the English–German school, by Saint-Simon and Comte, and by Carlyle. He expressed a respect for tradition and concern that its treasures not be lost; he accepted the idea of historical development; and he adopted paternalist and elitist positions. He was always strongly in favour of moral education, believing it to have virtually unlimited power to promote good, observing: 'the power of education is almost boundless: there is not one natural inclination which it is not strong enough to coerce, and, if needful, to destroy by disuse' (*Utility of Religion*, 1st ed., in *Three Essays on Religion*, p. 82 see *Collected Works*, x (Toronto and R.K.P.) p. 409). This, when combined with his associationist psychology, made it impossible for him to draw the kind of distinction vital to contemporary liberalism, between genuine education and mere indoctrination; and when associated with the sympathetic attitude expressed in *Utility of Religion* towards moral education to foster the Religion of Humanity construed as utilitarianism, and in *Utilitarianism* with the inculcating of utilitarian feelings, Mill was seriously exposed to the danger of becoming (what he for a brief time became) a moral totalitarian. Mill had a great distrust of state control with a state monopoly of education and seemed to think of it as being the area in which parents will exercise control, apparently not noticing that the alternative to state control may be control by religious and political groups, i.e. decentralised moral and political education which could be little more than indoctrination.

It is not possible here to trace out Mill's various complex views; instead, his dominant views on major issues will be examined. Mill's concern in most of his political writings was to state and defend a liberal democratic view of the state and society, and his writings therefore relate to a relatively small range of issues in political philosophy. Thus, while he was concerned to examine the problem of the proper role of the state, he was more deeply interested in defining the limits to legitimate interference with the individual's liberty by the state and society; while he argued that representative government was the ideal form of government, most of his writings concerning it relate to problems involved in making it such; similarly, in his other discussions relating to equality, equal rights for women and socialism, his context is very much that of an acceptance of a liberal view of society.

Method in the Social Sciences

As noted in chap. 2, Mill in the *Logic* (vi, 9 and 10) developed a theory of method in the social sciences in terms of what he called the concrete deductive and inverse deductive methods, being indebted to Comte for the latter method. Using these methods Mill sought to ground the empirical laws and looser generalisations on psychological laws. The importance of Mill's writings here lies not in the specific methods he outlined – they are of only very limited value – but in his, following Comte and yet to a large extent independently of him, raising the question of method and attempting to found a science of sociology, ethology and a philosophy of history. His attempts to found sociology on psychology have come in for a good deal of criticism, and the substantial progress that has been made in sociology has been largely a result of disregarding Mill's proposed programme.

Critics have objected to Mill's approach on the grounds that the laws governing individuals in groups are different from those governing individuals in isolation, and that Mill's methods involve a failure to appreciate this. This need not be the case. Mill clearly

98

noted that people are affected by their social environment, by other people, and by their social situations, and he saw part of the problem of sociology as springing from this fact. Clearly, whether or not individuals behave differently when alone, in mobs, or in organised social groups, there must be psychological as well as sociological explanations of their behaviour. Where Mill's approach is open to criticism is in his underestimating the influence of groups on individual behaviour, and hence the value of sociological laws by contrast with psychological laws. This is related to his uncritical acceptance of a belief in a common, universal human nature, at least in the sense of a nature governed by universal laws of the mind, by reference to which past and present social developments were to be explained.

Mill used his own methods in the social sciences much less than might have been expected. Thus, while we find that he sometimes carefully investigated the relevant facts, and while he appreciated fully the careful investigations of others, for example de Tocqueville, he was often, as in *Liberty* and in many discussions of aspects of the workings of democracy and socialism, content to rely on crude, impressionistic, unscientific, empirical generalisations which he did not attempt to confirm by reference to the concrete or inverse deductive methods.

Mill's Rationalism and Idealism

In spite of his being influenced by Coleridge, and his acceptance of cautious gradualism in introducing universal suffrage, Mill was in no sense a philosophical conservative. Indeed, some of his most unsympathetic, severest strictures, for example concerning Hume, were directed against conservatives. Mill saw the state and political change as being subject to human control which, when rationally planned on the basis of well-conceived ideals, was highly desirable; i.e. as against the philosophical conservatives, he thought rational

99

planning to be the proper course to adopt, provided due heed be given to the prudential considerations against state intervention. This is qualified by his acceptance of a theory of historical development, but since he accepted that his was a transitional society, this theory had no important, practical implications in respect of his major contentions. Mill's flexible, careful, thoughtful, non-doctrinaire rationalism, e.g. in respect of democracy and socialism, is itself proof of the inaccuracy and irrelevance of much contemporary conservative criticism of rationalism in politics. Mill's rationalism, although based on a concern to protect and realise various ideals, especially liberty, was not an *a priori* rationalism, but rather an approach to social organisation and planning on the basis of rational reflection about the relevant ideals and ascertained facts and laws. Such a rationalism has nothing to fear from criticisms by conservatives such as Burke and Oakeshott, for their criticisms derive what force they have from irrationalist attempts to organise society without regard to the known facts and on the basis of oversimplified theories.

Being a rationalist, Mill was also an idealist; indeed his rationalism was based on his idealism. He never seriously questioned but often stressed the power of an idea in the mind of a political reformer: 'One person with a belief is a social power equal to ninety-nine who have only interests' and 'It was not by any change in the distribution of material interests, but by the spread of moral convictions, that negro slavery has been put to an end in the British Empire and elsewhere ... It is what men think that determines how they act' (*Representative Government*, Everyman ed., pp. 183–4). Mill nowhere discussed theories such as those of Hegel and Marx in this connection, probably being unaware of Marx's dialectical and historical materialism. He did discuss the view that 'sinister', i.e. class interests, contrary to the general interest, must prevail, dismissing it, but the view of social change as resulting from economic causes in the Marxian sense of 'economic' was not discussed. Further, while like Bentham and James Mill he was aware of the dangers of ruling classes pursuing their own interests, and although he was aware of the need to check sinister interests, Mill appeared to believe that it had been empirically established that classes can and do rise above class interests and support measures contrary to their class interests, observing of the ruling class of his day that 'nor do I believe that any rulers in history have been activated by a more sincere desire to do their duty towards the poorer portion of their countrymen' (*Representative Government*, p. 209). Thus, even though aware of clashes, and of some of the dangers from clashes of class interests, Mill's discussions of class interests read as very pre-Marxian and superficial; he saw the rising working class as a greater source of danger than the capitalist and middle classes, and hence his preference for a gradualism in extending the franchise. Even though the Marxian account of the class struggle has not been borne out in all its details, it contains sufficient important truths, for example concerning the strength of the bourgeoisie and the difficulties of the working classes even when the latter have formal political power, to reveal that Mill took too optimistic a view of the facts he noted. In particular, he did not consider seriously enough how, in spite of individual goodwill, classes may, and may be obliged by economic circumstances to press class interests in order to secure their survival. Further, Mill seemed not to have appreciated the dangers of unconstitutional, revolutionary action, not by the workers but by the ruling classes resisting reforms. In general, his approach was that of a man who had never had to fight for his existence, of one who had never lived in the jungle of commerce of his day.

The Province of Government

Although he was a liberal, distrustful of state power, Mill was also a utilitarian, aware of how much the state could achieve. Hence his writings specifically on the province of government contain no unrealistic attempts to minimise the importance of government, nor any attempts to restrict the authority of the State to the single test of preventing 'force and fraud'. Rather, he took an ideal utilitarian standpoint, that the state should so act that its actions led to a maximising good. However, he saw this as involving a good deal of indirect action, and even inaction, on the part of the state, believing that other agencies and private individuals themselves are often better equipped to bring about many goods. None the less his account of the function of government is basically one in terms of the government achieving those goods it can, when and where the goods cannot more effectively or with less loss of goods such as liberty, individuality and self-development, be achieved by lesser agencies. For Mill, one of the most important goods with which the State should be concerned was the moral and spiritual well-being of its citizens, this however being seen by him as a good which is rarely to be fostered by coercive action.

In the *Political Economy*, Mill distinguished the necessary and the optional functions of government, the former being those inseparable from the idea of a government, or those habitually and without objection exercised by governments, while the optional functions are those about which there may be disagreement whether the government should exercise them. He rejected the views that the sole function of government is preservation of law and order, or the protecting of the community against force and fraud, noting instead the 'multifarious character of the necessary functions of government', the justification of which is 'the comprehensive one of general expediency' (v, 1, 2). In chaps 10 and 11 of the same book, Mill developed the view that there is a *prima facie* presumption in favour of the *laissez-faire* view, but that it is subject to a large number of qualifications which he proceeded to note. At the same time he never ruled out the possibility of a socialist social order, provided it could come to terms with the claims of liberty. Part of Mill's attempt to bring his considered view and that of *laissez-faire* individualistic liberalism into closer harmony proceeded by reference to a distinction between authoritative and non-authoritative intervention; he argued that the former, involving as it does directives and penalties, needs far greater justification than does non-authoritative intervention, the latter consisting as it did for Mill in the providing of facilities, the giving of advice, information and finance. (The examples cited include an established church, a state post office and a national bank, where other churches, private messenger services and private banks are also permitted.)

Much the same general view is to be found in Mill's other major political writings, *Representative Government, Liberty, Bentham,* and also in *The Utility of Religion.* In *Representative Government* special stress is laid on the importance of government providing conditions conducive to good character and personal traits. In *Liberty* Mill was not explicitly concerned with the question of the role of the State but with that concerning the proper limits to the State's, society's and the individual's right to interfere with the liberty of the individual. None the less, subject to qualifications to be discussed in the next section, this same view is consistent with Mill's considered conclusions in *Liberty*. It was no doubt because he was aware of this that he saw and presented his problem in *Liberty* as that of bringing together his utilitarianism and his liberalism, in chap. 1 indicating that his defence of liberty would be grounded on its utility. As the argument develops, it emerges that it is utility in the largest sense, that of an ideal utilitarianism encompassing as goods moral traits, integrity, moral goodness, individuality, self-development, as well as knowledge, rationality, rational and vital belief. It was because he believed that these goods are most usually fostered in an atmosphere of liberty that his ideal utilitarianism did not lead him to the authoritarian conclusions that many ideal utilitarians who held this view of the state have reached. Thus there is an overall consistency in Mill's accounts of the role of the State, and in these and his defence of liberty.

Without question Mill's most influential writing today is *On Liberty*. It promises to live up to Mill's expectation, expressed in the *Autobiography*, that it is likely to survive longer than any other of his works. Its fame rests on the widespread belief that in it Mill stated in a clearer, more definitive way than any previous writer, including Locke in his *Letter on Toleration*, and Milton in his *Areopagitica*, and more satisfactorily than has any writer since his day, the case for respecting the liberty of the individual. At the same time he is believed by many to have set out clear principles (or a clear principle) defining the limits to legitimate interference with the individual's liberty. The view for which Mill is celebrated is that it is never right to interfere with purely self-regarding actions, but only with harmful other-regarding ones, and then not always, while in respect of liberty of expression he demanded the fullest freedom. Mill's enterprise in *Liberty* is clearly one of the greatest importance; and although it will be argued here that he was less successful than his admirers commonly suggest, his contributions in *Liberty* are none the less substantial.

Mill's manner of approaching the problem of the limits of liberty makes for difficulty in expounding and assessing his views. He nowhere seriously explored the concept of liberty with which he operated, but gave a number of definitions, including the two – 'the only freedom which deserves the name, is that of pursuing our own good in our own way' (Everyman ed., p. 75) and 'for liberty consists in doing what one desires' (p. 152) – neither of which is that with which he operated in *Liberty*, for there he argued for the liberty to pursue one's evil and ultimate self-deterioration, and he obviously did not accept as free the person who freely entered into a slave contract and thereafter did only what he desired. Similarly, the definition with which he operated was not the negative concept of being let alone, but the more positive one of liberty as consisting in determining one's own conduct, being in control of one's destiny. Mill's writings on liberty also pose difficulties of interpretation because of a lack of definiteness as to when he sought to claim that legal restrictions are unjustified, and when he was making the larger claim, that both social and legal restrictions are illegitimate. In the Introduction to *Liberty* Mill suggested that he proposed to consider both, but it is evident in later chapters, as well as in other writings (*Letters, The Utility of Religion*), that there are important areas in which he simply wished to condemn legal prohibitions and to approve social sanctions, for example, to discourage capricious divorce and irresponsible procreation, although concerning the latter he was uncertain whether merely social sanctions could safely be relied upon. Another source of uncertainty springs from the fact that Mill seldom made clear whether and when he meant to indicate a necessary, when a sufficient, and when a necessary and sufficient condition for interference. He obviously aspired to set out what were necessary and sufficient conditions for interference to be legitimate, and much of the time he wrote as if a meaningful, relevant distinction could be drawn between self- and other-regarding actions such that purely self-regarding actions could never legitimately be interfered with, and hence that being other-regarding was a necessary condition for legitimate interference. Yet Mill modified even this claim, allowing that individuals may properly be coerced into rendering services to the state when engaged in purely self-regarding conduct.

While concerned to state a clear and determinate principle which indicated the legitimate limits to interference with the liberty of the individual, Mill did not wish to set the same limits to freedom of expression as to other kinds of action. He here explained himself as arguing for the 'fullest liberty of professing and discussing ... any doctrine' (*Liberty*, p. 78 n.). Even here he went on to allow a number of grounds for interference, namely, when the circumstances in which the views are expressed are such 'as to constitute their expression a positive instigation to some mischievous act'. (p. 114). He also allowed as legitimate, interference with acts, and hence, in consistency, utterances which are indecent, offensive, or breaches of good manners; and he entertained very seriously the view that it may be right for the State to curtail the freedom of expression of those who have an interest in making financial profit from the weakness of others, as in persuasively encouraging them to gamble, use prostitutes, etc. Mill's recognition of the right of the State to protect the individual against fraud would involve further limitations of freedom of expression. Mill nowhere stated a principle of freedom of expression designed to incorporate such interferences as these which he deemed to be desirable. Instead, when not explicitly noting the legitimate interferences, he wrote as if there ought to be unlimited freedom of expression.

Mill's Principles Concerning Liberty of Action

Mill indicated a number of distinct principles setting out the legitimate and illegitimate interferences. The best known is *the self- and other-regarding formula* which Mill stated thus:

> The individual is not accountable to society for his actions, in so far as these concern the interest of no person but himself. Advice, instruction, persuasion, and avoidance by other people if thought necessary by them for their own good, are the only measures by which society can justifiably express its dislike or disapprobation of his conduct. Secondly, that for such actions as are prejudicial to the interests of others, the individual is accountable, and may be subjected either to social or to legal punishment, if society is of opinion that the one or the other is requisite for its protection.

> In the first place, it must by no means be supposed, because damage, or the probability of damage, to the interests of others, can alone justify the interference

106

of society, that it therefore does justify such interference.

(*Liberty*, pp. 149–50; see also pp. 73, 75, 132, 133;
Political Economy, v 11, 2)

Mill here, as elsewhere, wrote as if purely self-regarding conduct can in fact and in principle be distinguished from other-regarding conduct such that it is
never right for the State, society, or for other individuals to interfere with purely self-regarding conduct.
He has also been construed, I suggest rightly although
subject to some qualifications, as taking joint action
between consenting adults, where the action harms no
third party, as self-regarding action. Thus he has been
taken as implying that homosexual actions between
consenting adults, fornication with security from repro-
duction, and the like are, although interpersonal, still
self-regarding acts. (Compare *Liberty*, p. 157, with the
discussions of prostitution, organised gambling and
trade as a social activity in the same chapter.)

An importantly different principle, which Mill and
others have treated as being identical with this, and
which may for brevity be characterised *the anti-paternalist principle*, is to the effect that it is never right to
coerce a man for his own good: 'his own good, either
physical or moral is not a sufficient warrant', and 'each
is the proper guardian of his own health, whether
bodily *or* mental and spiritual' (*Liberty*, pp. 73, 75).
That this is a distinct principle and not the statement
of a reason underlying the self- and other-regarding
principle is evident both from the fact that it does not
provide a ground for accepting the latter principle,
and because it condemns a different range of interferences, admitting interferences the latter explicitly condemns, for example coercion of a person engaged in
self-regarding actions in order to make him render services to others. This anti-paternalist principle is silent
about such interferences; the self-regarding principle
explicitly condemns them. (Mill implausibly sought to
justify such interference on the latter principle as
really preventing harmful other-regarding actions, that

'a person may cause evil to others not only by his actions but by his inaction, and in either case he is justly accountable to them for the injury' (p. 74); he also argued that to receive the protection of society renders the recipient liable to bear his share of the labours and sacrifices incurred in defending society or its members. The former makes nonsense of the distinction between self- and other-regarding actions; the latter acknowledges a duty which may be exacted contrary to that principle but not to the anti-paternalist principle. A person who fails to help another who is drowning because he is fishing, and the fish biting well, is acting in a purely self-regarding way, even though he thereby allows avoidable harm to come to another.) Mill indicated other principles, for example, in terms of self-protection, assignable duties. The two already noted are the important ones, and those most closely associated with Mill's name.

It was the self- and other-regarding principle which provoked the criticisms of his contemporaries, of James Fitzjames Stephen in *Liberty, Equality, Fraternity*, and of most critics since, the major criticism being that no actions are purely self-regarding, that all affect others. It was at least in part concern at the apparently damaging nature of this criticism that led Mill's followers and sympathisers, from John Morley to J. C. Rees and others today, to seek to reinterpret Mill's principle. Morley sought to make little of indirect, remote effects of actions, while Rees makes much of the distinction between simply affecting and adversely affecting the *interests* of another. Neither suggestion circumvents the criticism, nor is either consistent with Mill's own application of his principle. Morley's move fails for obvious reasons (Mill saw that the remote effects of procreation, colonisation, socialism must be taken into account), while Rees's suggestion is unsuccessful because Mill had no clear concept of interests, and also because Mill both did not confine legitimate interference to other-regarding actions which harmfully affect the interests of others, and would not have countenanced interference with many (self-regarding) actions which adversely affected the interests of others. (Letting one's house run to seed may seriously affect the financial interests of a neighbour who is seeking to sell his house.) See John Morley's 'Mr Mill's Doctrine of Liberty', *Fortnightly Review*, 1 Aug 1873, and J. C. Rees, 'A Re-reading of Mill on Liberty', *Political Studies*, VIII (1960) 113–29.

Mill's contentions here have commonly but wrongly been construed as a defence of the ideal of privacy. To be free from interference in one's self-regarding actions is distinct from having one's privacy respected; a person's privacy may be invaded without interfering with him, and without there being any attempt to promote his good, indeed, without the idea of coercion being relevant. The invader of privacy may act in secret and the self-regarding conduct of the individual be unaffected by the invasion of his privacy because he is unaware of it. Typically we are aware if we are subject to interference and coercion. Different arguments are also needed to support a demand for privacy than those for freedom from interference in respect of one's self-regarding actions.

Other criticisms have related to the exceptions which must be allowed if and when clear criteria of self-regarding actions are indicated. Other criticisms again have related to Mill's claim concerning other-regarding actions, difficulties arising from the fact that, while Mill suggested that only harmful other-regarding actions may be interfered with, he did not accept the fact that an action was both harmful and other-regarding as either a sufficient or a necessary condition for legitimate interference. He argued that it is illegitimate for the State or society to interfere with certain classes of harmful self- and other-regarding actions (for instance, where the harm is due to the influence of example, or to fair competition); he also allowed as legitimate interferences with certain classes of self-regarding actions as noted above. In order therefore to understand and assess Mill's account of the limits of liberty, it is necessary to appreciate how he saw his principles, and also the nature and grounds of the exceptions he allowed to them. When so understood, Mill's account emerges as being much more realistic, sensible and non-doctrinaire than the accounts attributed to him both by his self-proclaimed followers and by his critics.

Mill's use of his principles of liberty is on first sight puzzling. He stated them as if they are principles which apply universally in societies of civilised peoples, and admit of no exceptions. Yet he acknowledged innumerable exceptions. The truth of the matter is that he thought that the principles had a general utilitarian justification, and hence that there was a presumption in favour of determining interferences by reference to them. However, when clear ideal utilitarian considerations (which took full note of liberty and its goods) dictated exceptions, he was generally prepared to admit the exceptions. What is less satisfactory is that Mill was less systematic in his approach than this account suggests, and was at times somewhat arbitrary both in the exceptions he allowed and in those he rejected. In particular, he did not bring the arguments with which he supported his demands for liberty closely to bear on the detailed applications of his theory. But then, as Sir Isaiah Berlin has observed, the argument of *Liberty* is not its most valuable feature. It will therefore be useful to look now at the applications and exceptions Mill indicated to the above principles, for they, more than anything else, bring out the difficulties in the way of the realisation of the liberal hope that one day a satisfactory principle indicating either necessary and/or sufficient conditions for legal or social interference will be formulated.

(a) *Interferences with purely self-regarding actions for the sake of the good of the individual coerced.* Here Mill admitted to be legitimate interference to prevent accidents, his illustration being that of preventing a person crossing an unsafe bridge *where it is certain* that the bridge will collapse (*Liberty*, p. 152). Coercion in respect of education is also admitted, not, as later liberals have argued, as a means of enlarging liberty, but as an interference for the good of the person

110

coerced. This was qualified by a warning concerning the dangers of state control of education. (See *Political Economy*, v, 11, 8 and 9; also D. G. Ritchie, *Natural Rights*, chap. viii, esp. p. 138.) The context suggests that in any matter of importance in which the individual is not a competent judge of the commodity, the question of protecting him from the consequences of his uninformed judgements *may arise*. Mill did not here extend the application of this rule to self-medication (although he seems to have done so in *Hamilton* when discussing responsibility and punishment). He also allowed that the State or society may restrain, and in certain cases prevent, an individual who is engaged in purely self-regarding conduct from entering into an irrevocable contract; in *Liberty* he insisted that the State should in no way support or enforce a contract of slavery; in the *Political Economy* he explicitly stated his position as relating to all serious, irrevocable contracts (*Political Economy*, v, 11, 10). In effect Mill here accorded the State the right to prevent the individual engaged in purely self-regarding actions from entering into such irrevocable contracts as slave, wage and certain Christian marriage contracts with the backing of the law. His argument entails that suicide may also be legitimately prevented on at least some occasions, if this is possible.[1] In a letter to Harriet, Mill also approved the use of social pressure to discourage the joint self-regarding action of divorce by mutual consent, i.e. where no other party is harmed. He also

[1] Mill, in his discussion of religious suicides in his *Memorandum of the Improvements in the Administration of India during the Last Thirty Years, and the Petition of the East-India Company to Parliament* (London, Cox & Wyman, 1858; reprinted Farnborough, England, Gregg International Publishers, 1968), seems to confirm this by his approval of laws forbidding such suicides. He approvingly observed, for example: 'Various other modes of self-immolation practised in India – by drowning, burying alive, or starvation – have been, with equal success, prohibited and suppressed' (p. 49). He was, as he observed on p. 47, discussing the 'barbarous usages of the natives' of India, i.e. people who, in his eyes, were uncivilised. Even so, such approval of state-interference with what would often be purely private religious and personal conduct reads as illiberal.

accepted the legitimacy of coercing some (who are engaged in self-regarding actions) for the sake of mutually beneficial joint action, for example to obtain better labour conditions. This could equally be construed as coercion of the individual for his own good, but it need not always be that, and may be contrary to his own interest. These actual and implied exceptions to the self- and other-regarding and anti-paternalist principles are important exceptions; many would have been unacceptable to *laissez-faire* liberals such as Humboldt and Spencer. They are readily intelligible on the utilitarian interpretation of Mill's account of liberty.

(b) *Interferences with purely self-regarding actions to promote goods or to prevent evils.* The example of coercion to enforce the rendering of services to the community, taxation, military and jury service, appearing as a witness, etc., has already been alluded to. The interference by taxation, when taken in conjunction with Mill's acceptance of the use of this revenue to finance goods such as 'state charity', culture, research, exploration, and other goods which are not the specific concern of any one individual or group, is not a negligible one (*Political Economy*, v, 11, 14, 15). Mill showed awareness of this when in *Liberty* and elsewhere he expressed a strong preference for private enterprise providing services because of the great evil of adding unnecessarily to the government's power, and because of the educative value involved in individuals rather than the government engaging in enterprises such as providing roads, railways, banks, insurance offices, universities and the like. Mill also approved the use of coercion to make individuals engaged in purely self-regarding actions render services to prevent injury to others, here having in mind the helping of those who are being criminally assaulted. His contention none the less admits of quite wide application, and extensive interference with liberty. Mill also allowed, indeed enjoined, interference with the self-regarding actions of private and public cruelty to animals (the hurt to the spectator is comparable

112

with the hurt to the Moslem who is affronted by the eating of pork, a hurt Mill dismissed as irrelevant). Yet such interference may seriously thwart the self-development of those such as bull-fighters, hunters and the like, who are thereby prevented from pursuing their callings (*Political Economy*, v, 11, 9). Mill also approved of interference with those self-regarding actions which, when performed in public, are deemed to be offensive or indecent. His ground, no doubt, was that the observers are hurt; yet this was a ground he rightly rejected as inadequate when considering Sabbatarian legislation, and when commenting on the eating of pork before Moslems. While accepting the right to self-medication, Mill did acknowledge the need to prevent harm by way of accidents due to the taking of poisons in error; he therefore suggested that the chemist may properly be compelled to put warning labels on bottles. (This could equally be treated as interference with the other-regarding activity of trade.) Mill also saw no objection to interference to prevent crimes, yet the potential criminal may be engaged in purely self-regarding actions, e.g. getting drunk before driving, going for a stroll 'to case' a bank. Interference to prevent crimes is obviously reasonable on utilitarian grounds, but it admits of dangerous, undesirable applications. One of the most significant differences between liberal and totalitarian communities lies in how far and in what ways this interference is applied. Also, as Russell noted, the threat to liberty and its goods from the police is not one of the least serious threats to liberty in the modern liberal society. The common criticism that Mill, in allowing interference to prevent crimes, thereby allowed interference with any action at all, since a state may declare any kind of action to be criminal, is unfounded; Mill denied that states are entitled to declare any acts at all to be crimes. Mill also allowed as legitimate interference with the self-regarding actions of colonists acting in concert, the interference being said to be justified to prevent harm or to protect future generations. Again, these are significant interferences which Mill admitted,

113

interferences which an unqualified exponent of his principles would not be expected to admit.

(c) *Interference with harmful other-regarding actions*. Mill here indicated his view by reference to interferences which are not legitimate, those which are doubtful, and those others which are not of these types and which seemingly are legitimate.

(i) *Interference which is not legitimate*. Mill noted that where harm to others resulted from fair competition, as with examinations, professional competition, etc., the harm is not a sufficient reason for interference. However, his entertaining of the case for socialism reveals that, if the harm is great enough seriously to interfere with individuality and self-development, and the interference by the state less, the latter may be justified. Mill also insisted that harm caused by one's example (whether engaged in public self- or other-regarding actions, for example in getting drunk, taking drugs, engaging in adultery) is no ground for interference. Stephen here attacked Mill, citing the profligate aristocrat who encourages the debasement of marriage in 'the lower classes' by having mistresses in various cities. Mill might have sought to have replied to Stephen's criticism that the aristocrat's example causes harm only because those who follow it freely chose to do so, that the example is no more causally determining of their behaviour than a speech in favour of free love. This may, but need not always, be true. Those who are harmfully affected may not be mature, responsible persons; they may be children, or near-compulsive teenage imitators. Today it is often the unformed teenager who is harmed by his idol's example of drug-taking or irresponsible sexual behaviour. In Stephen's example, those most harmed are the innocent wives and children of those corrupted by the aristocrat's example. Here, as elsewhere in *Liberty*, Mill wrote as if members of civilised societies are completely rational and responsible, and this although elsewhere he showed often enough that he knew that they are not. Yet if they are not completely rational and responsible, the harm done by examples is very

114

relevant when determining which interferences are justifiable. Any responsible person who sets an example for no adequate reason which he knows will be followed by impressionable, immature persons, must accept some responsibility for the harm done to and by those who follow his example. While Mill also noted that trade is a social activity, and while he entertained the possible desirability of some socialistic interference with it, he so argued that it is not a proper object of interference except to prevent fraud, e.g. by adulteration of the commodity, to insist on sanitary precautions, to protect workers in dangerous occupations and the like.

(ii) *Interferences with other-regarding actions concerning which Mill expressed doubt.* Mill expressed uneasiness concerning the *laissez-faire* attitude towards gaming-house keepers, pimps, brothel owners and, by implication, prostitutes. This is surprising in view of his acknowledgement that 'whatever it is permitted to do, it must be permitted to advise to do', and the fact that the activities are freely entered into by all parties, no undue pressure (other than play upon weakness) being used, and that similar trading agreements, disadvantageous to certain parties, are accepted as properly immune from interference. The special treatment of trading in liquor suggests the same doubt, namely, that these may be cases where protection of the individual for his own good is justified. Mill's doubt here is also important as it springs from him according the state and society the right and competence to judge what is evil.

(iii) *Interferences with other-regarding actions which involve harm to others where Mill favoured interference.* It would seem that Mill accepted the fact that an other-regarding action had harmful effects as a *prima facie* ground for interference if it did not fall into one of the groups indicated in (i) and (ii) above. What is interesting is how far Mill was prepared to go in this area. Thus we find that he allowed considerable interference with what are now regarded as basic marriage and family rights, this chiefly on the basis of an economic theory that the condition of the workers could only permanently be bettered if the population was stabilised. Thus in the *Political Economy* he urged as a *prima facie* objection to various measures of social justice, including legally enforced minimum wages, that they would involve the paternalism of state interference with marriage and family rights to prevent overpopulation. None the less, earlier in the same section he had stated as a matter of principle that 'no one has the right to bring creatures into life, to be supported by other people' (*Political Economy*, II, 12, 2; see also *The Claims of Labour*, in *Dissertations and Discussions*, vol. II). In *Liberty*, Mill made more of the harm to the children who may be born of imprudent marriages, and was generally less apologetic, accepting such interference as legitimate if efficacious (p. 163). Applied today, Mill's proposal would amount to using social or, if that failed, legal enforcement of family planning on the basis of what the state or society deemed to be adequate economic resources of the parents, those with moral scruples being punished if they had children not approved by the State or society. To all but extreme Platonists this would represent an intolerable invasion of liberty, yet it is, on utilitarian grounds, proposed by Mill as part of his account of liberty. Mill also accepted coercion to enforce assignable duties, his contention here following naturally from his account of obligation. His discussions in *Utilitarianism* and *Liberty* suggest that an assignable duty was any duty to another person or persons which could be attributed to a specific moral agent, such a duty being of its nature one that it is useful to enforce. Few liberals today would wish to encourage such extensive interference. There are many assignable duties, e.g. of children to elderly parents, spouse to spouse, which ought not, legally or socially, to be enforced, albeit that it is desirable to encourage their performance.

In brief, Mill's illustrations and principles reveal that his is not an immunities thesis, that there are certain areas of a man's life, or certain kinds of actions, which are always without exception immune from legitimate interference. He allowed that purely self-regarding conduct may legitimately be interfered with, on occasions and subject to conditions not systematically formulated, but of an ideal utilitarian character, to protect or promote the individual's own good, and the good of others; to protect other persons and even animals from harm, entertaining inclusion within the former of the harm of corruption by parties who have financial interests in corrupting them. He condemned much coercion of the individual for his own good, and for the good of others, and even to prevent certain kinds of harmful actions. Thus Mill advanced neither a *laissez-faire* non-interventionist view of the State, nor the kind of liberal theory so commonly attributed to him today, but a liberalism founded on a fallible ideal utilitarian calculus. Further, Mill did not insist that the State ought to be morally neutral but accorded it the competence and the right to make moral and value judgements, and to coerce individuals on the basis of them. Thus the State is accorded the right to determine and enforce what is an assignable duty: it can declare cruelty to animals to be evil and act to suppress this evil; and both the State and society are acknowledged to have the competence to determine which of the practices that play on the weakness of the consumer are evil.

A problem raised by Mill's critics, which he himself noted but did not fully appreciate, and which bears equally on social coercion of self- and other-regarding actions, relates to the distinction he drew between expressing displeasure at another's conduct and applying social pressure to make the person conform with the desired standards. Mill insisted that the former is permissible only when the conditions indicated in his principles and illustrations prevail, namely: 'I hold that it is allowable in all, and in the more thoughtful and cultivated often a duty, to assert and promulgate, with all the force they are capable of, their opinion of what is good or bad, admirable or contemptible, but not to compel others to conform to that opinion; whether the force used is that of extra-legal coercion, or exerts itself

117

by means of law' (*Political Economy*, v, 11, 2). And: 'A person who shows rashness, obstinacy, self-conceit – who cannot live within moderate means – who cannot restrain himself from hurtful indulgences – who pursues animal pleasures at the expense of those of feeling and intellect – must expect to be lowered in the opinion of others, to have less share of their favourable sentiments; but of this he has no right to complain, unless . . .' (*Liberty*, pp. 134–5). It is a basic liberty that we be free to express and, when no direct harm results, to act upon our moral disapprovals; at the same time we ought not socially to coerce others. Yet usually, social pressure and sanctions are not organised things, but the concomitance of individual approvals and disapprovals. Thus, to show that his distinction is relevant in practice, Mill needed to show how it could usefully be appealed to in the hackneyed example of the homosexual butcher who is bankrupted because his customers, as individuals, express their disapproval by switching their custom elsewhere. Unorganised social pressure is as serious a threat to liberty as organised social pressure. To seek a solution by arguing that, where our attitudes are shared by the majority of others, we ought not to express them, is to advocate unreasonable curtailment of expression and action. Mill did not so argue, but neither did he offer a solution to what is for all liberals a very real problem.

Mill's Arguments for Liberty

Mill advanced many important arguments, all being ideal utilitarian arguments, of the form that liberty is a means to, condition or ingredient of goods, and an intrinsic good in its own right, where the goods pointed to are true, rational and lively belief, individuality, self-development and progress. The arguments establish much that is important and true, although less than is claimed in the principles, and something rather different from what is suggested by Mill's illustrations of his view.

The infallibility argument that intolerance involves an unjustified claim to infallible knowledge, and hence may deprive mankind of access to true knowledge, is without doubt Mill's most important argument for freedom of expression, and is not without some importance as an argument for freedom of action (see *Liberty*, pp. 79–81). It is easy today to overlook the significance of this argument because it has been so successful; much intolerance in the past emanated from those who dogmatically and unjustifiedly believed themselves to possess infallible knowledge. The claim to infallible knowledge is now rarely made, yet it is not long since it was frequently and unashamedly made by many. It is probably to Mill and to his statement of this argument that we are in a large measure indebted for this improved state of affairs. The argument is further important because many other arguments draw on its premiss and conclusion. We distrust the interference of those who seek to guide the self-development of other adults, because they may be mistaken; we distrust state power, because it may be mistakenly applied and even abused; coercion of an individual for his own good shows lack of respect chiefly although not solely in so far as it is misdirected.

As an argument to establish Mill's announced conclusion it is none the less inadequate. It rests on very questionable assumptions; and it purports to establish much more than it can and does. It is offered as a decisive argument against intolerance of expression (and of action based on the belief concerned) of all kinds of belief, but especially those of religion, morality, politics, aesthetics and tastes, but it is relevant only if cognitivist analyses of statements of these beliefs are true, for the core of the argument is the claim concerning the value of truth. The argument also presupposes a judgement concerning the relative values of the truth and other goods; in so far as it is offered as an argument for unlimited freedom of expression, it presupposes that the value of true belief outweighs the values of all those goods which are lost or jeopardised by freedom of expression. It further assumes that we can never possess certainty in the absence of a context of discussion. Again, argument is needed to show that we do not have infallible knowledge; for example, that it is wrong to inflict pointless suffering on innocent persons. More basically, it is not true that, to be justified in restricting freedom of expression, we must lay claim to infallible knowledge. Mill, in effect, acknowledged this in his restriction on inflammatory speech. His statement of the argument suggests that any restriction of freedom of expression has world-wide repercussions; this can be so, but often what is denied free expression in one country enjoys favoured treatment in another. Also there are kinds and degrees of restriction of free expression, with total suppression being relatively uncommon. Many empirical beliefs would not be lost if scope were denied to free discussion; on the other hand, the existence of other beliefs does not depend on there being freedom of communication. Thus, as stated by Mill, the argument rests on questionable assumptions and involves false claims. Its most serious shortcoming springs from the untenable value judgement on which it rests. The truth does not so outweigh all other values to the extent that it is never or seldom right to deny expression to a true belief in order to secure other goods. The argument has importance as pointing to one among other relevant, important considerations when assessing the case for freedom of expression and action.

Mill's second argument is that *freedom of expression (and action) is necessary for vital belief*, that, without such freedom, beliefs will be held as mere dead doctrines or beliefs. Mill's use of this argument is itself an answer to the persistent criticism that his defence of liberty is a defence of scepticism or indifferentism; Mill cared deeply about the truth and wished to see true beliefs held as vital, lively ones. However, because it rests on an oversimplified claim concerning the relevant empirical facts, this argument is less satisfactory than the infallibility argument. Tolerance and intolerance have varying effects, sometimes the one and sometimes the other leads to greater depth and vitality in the belief concerned. Mill also argued that *freedom of expression and discussion are necessary for rational belief*, that intolerance involves the danger of protected beliefs coming to be accepted without rational backing and hence in the manner of superstitions and prejudices. There is a good deal of truth in Mill's contention, although the nature and the extent of this danger depends greatly on the kind of truth concerned – compare here analytic and scientific truths with those of morals, politics, religion. Further, there is the counter-consideration that in a context of free discussion a plausible, unscrupulous propagandist may cause a rationally grounded, true belief to be abandoned for a false belief based on pure emotion. It is this argument, more than any, which exposed Mill to the damaging criticism that he had an exaggerated idea of the rationality of men, and of the level and character of public discussions.

Liberty as a Condition of Self-development

(i) Mill rightly noted that freedom of expression is important for self-development. To plan one's life wisely and well one needs information. Learning about different styles of life, different social orders, social institutions, allows one to seek to plan one's life in a more informed, more effective way. Also, as rational beings, the very expression, exchange and discussion of different views is itself an important part of self-development. None the less, freedom of expression may endanger self-development by encouraging false views, and when this is so, concern for self-development would dictate the necessary restrictions on expression and discussion. Although Mill saw that the people to whom he wished to accord the fullest freedom of expression were imperfectly rational, 'that the prospect of the future depends on the degree in which they [the labouring classes] can be made rational beings', he failed to draw the obvious conclusion that the case for freedom of expression from self-development must

121

always be judged in its specific context. In view of his concern about overpopulation, Mill might have seen this more clearly today in contexts in which religious propaganda against birth control proved to be successful. (ii) He argued for freedom of action from its being a condition and ingredient of individuality and self-development in various ways, namely: Liberty is a condition for experiments of living; it aids our self-development in that each is the best judge and guardian of his own interests; freedom of thought and action have great educative value; and there is, further, a suggestion of Humboldt's argument 'coercion may prevent many transgressions; but it robs even actions which are legal of a part of their beauty. Freedom may lead to many transgressions, but it lends to vice a less ignoble form' (*On the Limits of State Action*, C.U.P. ed., p. 80). This is associated with the claim that liberty is 'the only unfailing and permanent source of improvement'.

(*a*) *Experiments of living.* Mill argued that 'as it is useful that while mankind are imperfect there should be different opinions, so it is that there should be different experiments of living'. (*Liberty*, pp. 114–15). As an inductive logician Mill might reasonably have been expected to be using 'experiments' here metaphorically; in fact he appears to suggest that they are real experiments which bring true knowledge both to the experimenters and their observers. Experiments of living are not real experiments nor akin to such; there are and can be no satisfactory criteria for determining what constitutes a conclusive experiment of living. The conclusions which suggest themselves as true to the experimenter may appear so only because he has not engaged in other experiments; and they may be false for the observer. Consider here experiments of living in respect of sexual behaviour, and their value for the experimenters and their observers. Mill wrote as if it is possible to engage in a series of experiments without the very fact of doing so affecting the experimenter's reactions to and conclusions concerning other experiments. Some experiments are irreversible, e.g.

drug-taking; where reversible, the experiment may none the less involve damage to the experimenter's judgement. This is as true with large-scale social experiments concerning fascism, communism, socialism, prohibition, etc., as with personal experiments of living. Many of the more interesting social and personal experiments would be condemned by Mill as involving illegitimate interference with others. What is true in Mill's claim is that if all are free to engage in different modes of living, society may gain greater insight into the characters and values of different modes of life to a degree to which this would be unlikely without such diversity. To dignify this truth by speaking of experiments of living is extremely misleading. In advocating experiments of living, Mill came in effect to praise diversity, difference and eccentricity for themselves, and a society in which there is diversity as preferable to one in which there is uniformity. Stephen rightly commented here that a society which lacked diversity in having only sober citizens was preferable to one with the diversity of drunk and sober. Mill's love of difference did not extend to the smallest society, that of marriage, the ideal of which he saw to consist in a union of two persons 'of cultivated faculties, identical in opinions and purposes' (*Subjection of Women*, p. 311).

The appeal to the value of experiments of living is part of Mill's case for liberty as a condition and ingredient of self-development. Here what Mill needed to establish was that guided self-development may not be more successful than unguided experiments of living, that individuals will not be self-stultifying if left without guidance. Many are foolish, reckless, uninformed or deliberately misinformed and encouraged to act unwisely by others with an interest in their so acting; guidance and constraints may therefore contribute to a more successful self-development. Mill's supporting argument that 'each is the best judge and guardian of his own interests', and the argument concerning the educative value of freedom, do something to meet such a claim. At the same time they confirm what his unwillingness to accord liberty to the uncivilised, the immature and to lunatics confirms, namely that for Mill not any development is self-development; that self-development meant good self-development. This is further confirmed by his description of what is involved in a life of self-development – rationality in planning, self-control, firmness of character, etc. (*Liberty*, p. 117). Were liberty always to involve such admirable forms of self-development, the case for liberty from self-development would be very strong. In fact, many exercise their self-determination self-destructively, as with the weak-willed, the ditherer, the fool, the incompetent, the rash; others employ it to prey on the weakness of others, as with pimps, brothel owners, criminals; yet they too are engaged in 'experiments of living'.

(*b*) '*Each is the best judge and guardian of his own interests.*' Mill pressed this argument as part of his general case for liberty, that liberty is essential for an individual's self-development, in support of his demand for equal rights for women, and in his questioning of the claims of socialism and communism. As an argument for liberty it appears to run that, knowing and guarding our interests better than others, we shall, if we have the liberty to do so, pursue our interests and hence our self-development better than without such liberty. In the *Political Economy* he noted that it is subject to 'numerous abatements and exceptions'. Clearly this is so; the premiss is at best a rough generalisation and there are many areas, additional to those noted by Mill, in which the individual is either not the best judge or not the best guardian or neither in respect to his own interests. We may lack the knowledge to be the best judge or guardian of our own interests; we may lack the strength of character, or simply the political or social power, to guard our interests. We live in highly complex communities in which the actions and inaction of others may seriously impinge on our interests. Thus the argument holds where it holds; and this has to be determined in the concrete situation. At best it creates a *prima facie* presumption in favour of liberty, and even this is qualified by the fact acknowledged by Mill, namely, that it may be legitimate to override the individual's judgement in order to promote some good or goods other than his interests. Mill saw this in respect of poor laws, colonisation and government intervention to render services where private enterprise fails to do so, i.e. where general utilitarian considerations prudently weighed suggest this.

(c) *The educative value of liberty* is constantly stressed by Mill, in defence of freedom from interference in the *Political Economy* and *Liberty*, in supporting the universal franchise in *Representative Government*, equality for women in *The Subjection of Women*, and in assessing the claims of socialism and private property in the *Political Economy*. Thus in the *Political Economy* he wrote:

> The business of life is an essential part of the practical education of a people; without which, book and school instruction, though most necessary and salutary, does not suffice to qualify them for conduct, and for adaptation of means to ends.... A people among whom there is no habit of spontaneous action for a collective interest – who look habitually to their government to command or prompt them in all matters of joint concern ... have their faculties only half developed; their education is defective in one of its most important branches. (v, 11, 6)

This argument does not hold of all human beings, hence the accepted restrictions in respect of children and mental defectives. It is true that Mill accorded the right to liberty only to the civilised, mature minority of mankind, but unless he so interpreted these terms in ways which would make his theory irrelevant to any actual community, there are mature, civilised people whose education in life is better for their being guided by legal and social pressure. Indeed, education itself is generally more successful when supported by such pressure. Mill himself observed that 'to be held to rigid rules of justice for the sake of others, develops the feelings and capacities which have the good of others as their object' (*Liberty*, p. 121). The same awareness of the value of coercion in moral education, even of adults, is noted in *The Utility of Religion*. His contention is thus that restrictions for the sake of the self-development of others develop the coerced person's character.

Liberty as Conducive to Progress

In an extravagant passage Mill wrote of liberty as 'the only unfailing and permanent source of improvement'; he also argued from the evils coercive interference may involve. These can be construed as aspects of a more general, positive argument, that liberty is a condition for attaining goods. Whether improvement in fact follows from liberty depends on the society and its people. Mill saw this in respect of uncivilised peoples, including apparently the inhabitants of India of his day. Yet even in more advanced communities, liberty may jeopardise improvement – consider for example unstable, divided or underdeveloped communities; consider also the restrictions accepted as essential in wartime. Mill no doubt would reply here in terms of the long-term effects of liberty versus restrictions, but such a reply will not do, for what is required for improvement is the best combination of restrictions and liberty, as opposed to settling permanently for one or the other. It is of note that Mill offered no serious scientific evidence in support of this and other factual claims in his defence of liberty. Put negatively, that interference with liberty, far from leading to progress and improvement, is likely to result in serious evils, this argument is more convincing, although still subject to major qualifications. Mill stressed the dangers of interferences being misdirected, and the evil of adding unnecessarily to the power of the State (*Liberty*, pp. 133, 140, 165). Mill is clearly right that much interference, which renders the person who refuses to be constrained a criminal, is often misdirected and therefore doubly harmful; but there are areas, concerning expression and action, for example advocacy of racialism, lies about the effects of a very harmful or very useful commodity, coercion to prevent or reduce the seriousness of accidents, to secure education, and the like, where the State may and ought to interfere to protect the individual. Mill's argument has value chiefly in pointing to the need for caution in encouraging the State and society to interfere.

Liberty as an Intrinsic Good: Positive and Negative Liberty

In various places Mill appears to argue that liberty is of intrinsic value, that coercion of its nature is intrinsically evil. He observed that 'all restraint, *quâ* restraint, is an evil'. (*Liberty*, p. 150; see also pp. 115, 116, 138.) No doubt because he saw interferences as the threat to liberty, Mill is commonly interpreted as operating with a negative concept of liberty, with liberty viewed as consisting in not being interfered with, in being let alone (see I. Berlin's *Two Concepts of Liberty*). In fact his operative concept was that of self-determination. However, there are occasions on which Mill glimpsed a more positive concept which has since come to be of the greatest importance in liberal and socialist thought. Mill occasionally noted that lack of necessary conditions for effective self-determination, e.g. when impoverished, involved limitations on one's freedom. He observed, for example: 'the restraints of Communism would be freedom in comparison with the present condition of the majority of the human race'. (*Political Economy*, II, 1, 3.) Mill nowhere elucidated and developed the concept of liberty implied by this kind of observation, and it was left to later liberals, D. G. Ritchie, L. T. Hobhouse (more cautiously) and to socialists such as R. H. Tawney and H. J. Laski and others, to develop and employ the concept in support of coercive measures directed at improving conditions and thereby enlarging most people's effective range of choices.

Had Mill meant by liberty simply freedom from interference, being let alone, the claim that liberty is of intrinsic value could not be sustained. There is no intrinsic value in leaving alone, and free from interference, a blind man who is about to walk into the path of an oncoming truck. We value such negative liberty for the goods it makes possible, or because the securing of it secures its possessors from various evils, and not for its own sake. A careful reading of the writings of its more notable exponents, e.g. W. von Humboldt and Herbert Spencer, confirms this. If liberty is to be interpreted as self-determination, different objections arise. There is no special value in the liberty enjoyed by the aimless, shiftless drifter or the sadistic hunter; the situation would be better for the latter's actions not being freely chosen. Intrinsic value cannot properly be attributed to self-determination in the abstract; it is the complexes of which it is an element, the heroic acts, acts of thoughtful, creative self-development, and the like to which we attribute value. Thus the value of self-determination depends on how it is used; when used to seek good ends, rationally to promote goods such as self-development, the general happiness, to pursue knowledge, it is right to foster it; when used to pursue evil ends, no good is lost if coercion is used to prevent them. Mill often seemed to see liberty as consisting in good exercises of liberty, in one's being self-developing, or pursuing one's good ('The only freedom which deserves the name, is that of pursuing our own good in our own way'). So understood, it would be of intrinsic value.

In Brief

Mill did not succeed in setting out and defending a clear, determinate principle defining the limits of liberty. What he did succeed in doing was to point to general guiding principles concerning legitimate and illegitimate interferences, and to the kinds of applications and exceptions which might follow from weighing the claims of liberty and its goods, and those of goods other than liberty, although his discussion suffers from there being no systematic attempt to bring and think together the various applications with one another, and with the arguments used to support his demand for liberty. Many of Mill's illustrations and applications are both surprising and untenable, some because too illiberal, for example concerning marriage and procreation, others because too *laissez-faire* and libertarian. Some of Mill's untenable claims about interferences rest on mistaken factual beliefs; others spring from the limited range of values with which he operated, and from the fact that he operated with them in a less than systematic manner; others are due to the relative weightings he attributed to values such as liberty, self-development, knowledge, justice. Perhaps the most important shortcoming of Mill's discussion springs from the fact noted above that he only occasionally glimpsed but never explicitly accepted what so many later liberals have accepted as being of the utmost importance, namely, that the State can do much to enlarge an individual's effective enjoyment of his liberty. An effective national health service, in securing the good of health to many who would lack it, being crippled, confined to bed or doomed to early deaths, provides a condition which allows for greater, more effective exercise of liberty, more scope for individuality, and greater opportunities for effective self-development. Similarly with employment, money, news, legal aid and the like. The impoverished, unemployed person who, because he cannot secure work, suffers from malnutrition and disease, who would, if he could, marry the woman he loves, have a family, be creatively active in his chosen career as a builder, but who because of his poverty is unable to do any of these things, is a slave compared with the well-paid worker in the modern liberal welfare state; he is not truly free to be self-developing; the latter usually is.

Mill was far more egalitarian than most of his contemporaries, as is evident in his support of democracy with a universal franchise, his concern for equality for women, and his readiness to consider as sympathetically as he did the case for socialism. Indeed, his egalitarian demands, especially in respect of women, were among those least acceptable to his contemporaries. By mid-twentieth-century standards Mill was a qualified egalitarian, so much so that he has often recently been described as an elitist. Mill can only fairly be judged in the context of his time and, when so judged, emerges as one who accepted or entertained what are now widely regarded by liberal democrats as having been enlightened positions; the qualifications upon which he insisted, or which he simply considered, are such as still to merit some consideration today. It is none the less true that for him equality was a subordinate ideal; it had to be that in view of his defence of liberty. Further, various of his arguments here, like those of other egalitarians, admit of un- and anti-egalitarian implications.

Democracy

Unlike Locke and Rousseau, Mill was interested neither in whether democracy was the only legitimate form of government, nor in when it was legitimate. He accepted it as a fact, and as having claims in justice, and saw it as potentially the ideal form of government, his problem being how to make it in fact the ideal government, where by 'the ideal government' he meant that which 'if the necessary conditions existed for giving effect to its beneficial tendencies, would, more than all others, favour and promote not some one improvement, but all forms and degrees of it' (*Representative Government*, p. 201). Mill noted that representative government did not always measure up as the best government, for example, when the citizens were not interested in political affairs, when they were unable or unwilling to do what is necessary for its preservation, including fulfilling and discharging the duties it imposes. Mill's discussion here is a model of a careful, thoughtful use of a concept of an ideal political system, and contrasts with his discussion of the relative claims of socialistic and private property systems to be the ideal social orders. Here Mill noted that because representative government is the ideal form of government under ideal conditions, it does not follow that it should be aimed at when these conditions do not hold. Mill's unegalitarian proposals occur in his statement of the conditions necessary to render representative government (hereafter to be referred to as democracy) good government.

Two arguments are basic to Mill's defence of democracy. He argued that it makes possible greater self-dependence and may provide more scope for individuality and self-development than any other practicable form of government, and thus, other things being equal, must be preferred if tested thus: 'a government is to be judged by its action upon men, and by its action upon things; by what it makes of the citizens, and what it does with them; its tendency to improve or deteriorate the people themselves, and the goodness or badness of the work it performs for them, and by means of them' (*Representative Government*, p. 195). As the two essays *De Tocqueville on Democracy in America* bring out, Mill was aware that democracy simply made these goods possible, that, far from guaranteeing them, it may endanger their realisation. Except for a brief discussion of government by bureaucracy, Mill neglected to complete this argument by examining the claims of other systems of government to be capable of attaining the ideal standards, no doubt because he attached such great importance to the educative value of participation in democratic government, and because he believed it encouraged active rather than passive types. As J. A. Schumpeter has brought out, when actual democracies are examined, these hopes are not evidently realised (see *Capitalism, Socialism and Democracy*, chap. 21). The second argument, that the general and the individual's interest are best protected when all have the right to participate in the choosing of their rulers, is simply a restatement of the argument of Bentham and James Mill; it is supported by such claims as 'Each is the only safe guardian of his rights and interests', 'Human beings are only secure from evil at the hands of others in proportion as they have the power of being, and are, self-*protecting*; and they only achieve a high degree of success in their struggle with Nature in proportion as they are self-*dependent*, relying on what they themselves can do, either separately or in concert, rather than on what others do for them' (*Representative Government*, p. 208). In *The Rationale of Political Representation* he noted that men will always prefer their own interests when they compete with those of another. An important part of this argument relates to the need to bring about an identification of interest between the rulers and the ruled, Mill seeing in popular institutions a means of contributing to this identity of interest, and hence to the goods which come from it. However, as the essays *De Tocqueville on Democracy in America* bring out, Mill's contention was simply that democratic government may, not that it will, achieve this.

There is an argument from justice, Mill contending that it would be an injustice to withhold the suffrage unless there are grounds in terms of prevention of greater evils for doing so (*Representative Government*, p. 279). It was stated forcefully in *Thoughts on Parliamentary Reform* as 'there is no such thing in morals as a *right* to power over others; and the electoral suffrage is that power' (*Dissertations and Discussions*, III 21). Since Mill explained justice in terms of utility, this argument too becomes basically a utilitarian one in terms of the goods which may come from according a vote to all. This explains, too, Mill's readiness to restrict the franchise on utilitarian grounds.

Mill's arguments for democracy are therefore basically egalitarian. The unstated premiss, that each man's individuality, self-development, interests and rights are equally deserving of consideration, is thoroughly egalitarian and, like the similar egalitarian claim underlying the argument of *Liberty*, that each man's liberty is equally deserving of respect, it ultimately rests on ideal utilitarian considerations, that greater good generally comes from accepting and acting on this belief. Thus it is that Mill excluded, on utilitarian grounds, certain societies as unready for popular government; hence too his willingness to qualify his egalitarian demands when utility, widely conceived, dictates this. We therefore find in Mill's defence of democracy not a defence of equality in its own right, but equality as a means to or condition of other goods. This means that, if the factual claims of anti-egalitarians and anti-democrats, from Plato to the present time, can be substantiated, viz. that democracy cannot achieve the kinds of goods Mill claimed it to be capable of realising, his writings would offer no answer. This is a virtue, not a defect, for the strongest arguments for equality are not arguments for equality as such, nor even for equality from justice, but for equality as just because and in so far as it is dictated by utility. An examination of the common arguments for racial equality or, as will become evident from Mill's arguments, for equality of the sexes, reveals that the arguments from justice admit of anti-egalitarian conclusions just as fully as do the utilitarian arguments, if the facts turn out in the appropriate ways.

Mill made significant unegalitarian qualifications directed at avoiding misgovernment, seeing the dangers to good government as coming from class legislation, stupidity, and from pressures which threatened liberty and diversity. His chief qualifications were first in his attitude towards introducing universal franchise (here favouring gradualism), secondly in favouring plural votes for the educated and well informed, thirdly in favouring proportional representation, fourthly in denying votes to or restricting the votes of the illiterate or immoral (among whom he seemed to include the unemployed). He changed his views on the ballot, according as he judged the effects to be beneficial or harmful to the general interest; he similarly considered the pros and cons of a second chamber; he opposed payment of Members of Parliament; and he favoured a legislative commission to draft laws, and did much to foster and bring about an efficient public service with selection based on examination. Some of these proposals can be taken to reveal an anti-egalitarian, elitist tendency, yet when taken in their historical context, and with the exception of plural votes, they are scarcely that.

The favouring of gradualism is to be contrasted with the reluctance of the many to accept universal franchise: Mill was among the egalitarians in supporting it as strongly as he did, and as including female suffrage. It is his reason which is strange. He feared class legislation based on 'sinister interests', and feared that until the working class was more rational, educated and moral, universal suffrage would introduce the danger of working-class legislation. Mill's writings here read as naïve and pre-Marxian, he being totally unaware of the immense power which economically strong, political minorities may have even in democracies. In denying the vote to the illiterate, and in considering a moral test which would exclude, among others, those 'seen drunk during the previous year', Mill was simply seeking safeguards against misgovernment.

The more important proposals relate to plural votes and proportional representation. Neither of these seems likely to achieve the objects Mill sought. He had hoped that by giving everyone a vote, and the informed and educated (understood as Mill understood education) plural votes, a balance of interests would be created, and the numerical majority, the workers, would be unable to swamp the minority. He also seemed to think it just that the informed have a greater say. An examination of the class structure of a modern democratic state, of the voting patterns of the educated, their interest in and concern for political issues, and the locations of the power centres, would suggest that Mill's hopes were seriously misplaced. If the universities today had the right to elect Members of Parliament, it is unlikely that they would be more discriminating and perceptive than other electorates. The complex system of proportional representation outlined by Hare, which Mill favoured as a partial solution to the problem of securing an adequate hearing for minorities and minority points of view, and thereby also checking class legislation, appears to be of the kind used in the election of the Australian Senate today. There is much to be said for and against such a system, and the debate continues today. Such a system can never be a complete, nor a completely satisfactory, solution, and that which Mill favoured in *Liberty*, in terms of tolerance and respect for differing viewpoints, is more basic. Depending on the make-up of a community, whether it is politically unified or fragmented, it could be of value or positively dangerous to the stability and security of the community. At best, depending on the whims of the majority in parliament, it could bring about a hearing of those minority groups which succeed in having representatives elected; but where the minority does not hold the balance of power, the hearing may be of little practical value. At worst, it could give to an irresponsible minority the balance of power, and lead either to corrupt government and pandering to the interests of the minority group contrary to the national interest, or, where there are many minority groups, to instability and a breakdown of democracy. None the less Mill saw a real problem which democracies have yet to solve. His proposal in *Liberty* is the most promising one to date, dealing as it does with the pressure for uniformity and conformity which democracy generates, and which equally concerned de Tocqueville and Mill.

The Equality of Women

Mill's writings in support of political, legal and social equality for women, the most important of which is

The Subjection of Women, read today like a series of truisms, yet in his own time no other of his writings aroused such hostility, even so able and discerning an admirer and critic as James Fitzjames Stephen being outraged by Mill's endeavours here, and suggesting that his arguments verged on the indecent. The reason Mill's writings here seem so unimportant today is in no small measure due to Mill himself, to his helping to change public opinion; had he been re-elected to Parliament and lived longer, it is probable that equality of the sexes would have been achieved sooner and more widely. When Mill wrote, the political, legal and social disabilities of women were great, and evidently unjust and indefensible to us today. Mill was not guilty of a serious overstatement when he wrote that 'marriage is the only actual bondage known to our law' (*The Subjection of Women*, Everyman ed., p. 296; all subsequent references are to this edition). The freedom enjoyed by Mrs Taylor and other women was not by legal right but by courtesy of their husbands.

The arguments for equality of women are well known and need only a brief mention. Mill's case consisted of a number of positive arguments, for example, concerning the abuses of non-responsible power, the evils of subjection generally (these being reinforced by their usual support, 'that each is the best judge and guardian of his own interests'), and the claim in justice that those women who have equal abilities and capacities should have this fact acknowledged; and a number of negative arguments, either by way of refuting those of his opponents, or of an *ad hominem* character. Obviously the utilitarian arguments, from the abuses of power, the evils of subjection, from each being the best judge and guardian of his own interest, simply because of the arbitrariness of the allocation of power, have greater force and relevance here than elsewhere. (As Mill noted, women are neither lunatics, natural servants, children, nor fools.) The argument from justice is interesting and potentially anti-egalitarian, as Plato saw, for it is the very argument that Plato used to support equality of the sexes *and* the division into

136

classes in the *Republic*. Mill argued that women are naturally equal with men, that the observable differences in abilities are due to education and circumstances (p. 269), and that while they are generally suited to different jobs, some women are fit for political office; that 'as long therefore as it is acknowledged that even a few women may be fit for these duties, the laws which shut the door on these exceptions cannot be justified by any opinion which can be held respecting the capacities of women in general'. The negative and *ad hominem* arguments are of interest only as revealing the limitations of human objectivity and reason. Mill felt obliged to reply to arguments of able and intelligent opponents which today we should not accept as sincerely or seriously proposed.

Socialism, Communism and Economic Justice

Mill was never a socialist, but his writings did much to advance the cause of socialism, particularly Fabian Socialism. The *Autobiography* suggests that Mill became a socialist (see especially pp. 195–9, World Classics ed.). If the relevant writings are examined, namely the *Political Economy*, even the 2nd and 3rd editions, revised at Harriet Taylor's instigation, and the posthumous *Chapters on Socialism*, it is clear that in any contemporary sense of the term Mill was far from being a socialist, even though he had a feeling that, with the coming of the franchise, socialism may be inevitable. Mill's writings helped the cause of socialism, first because Mill took socialist and, to only a lesser degree, communist theories seriously, as theories to be reckoned with, observing of socialism in the 2nd edition of the *Political Economy* that it 'has now become irrevocably one of the leading elements of European politics' (iv, 7, 5), the theories with which he was concerned being Owenism, Fourierism and Saint-Simonianism, but not Marxism. Secondly, Mill, under the influence of Saint-Simon, rejected theories that property rights are inalienable and inviolable, accept-

137

ing instead their relativity, that many are of recent origin and such as to have various justifications, the right to the fruits of one's labour being the dominant one, prescription another. On this basis and as a means of eliminating extremes of inequality of wealth (as he thought, in two generations), Mill proposed severe restrictions on the rights of inheritance and bequest. In so questioning and challenging property rights in this way, Mill challenged one of the main grounds for opposition to socialist and communist theories, Thirdly, and on the basis of this, he approached the question of private property versus socialism purely on the basis of which best realised the goods which are to be realised. Here, by contrast with his discussion of equality of women, he did not start from any presumption in favour of equality, or any notion that inequalities need special justification. Rather, his dominant concern was whether socialism or private property would allow most scope for liberty, individuality and self-development; with socialism, 'the decision will probably depend mainly on one consideration, viz., which of the two systems is consistent with the greatest amount of human liberty and spontaneity'; with communism, whether 'there would be any asylum left for individuality of character; whether public opinion would not be a tyrannical yoke; whether the absolute dependence of each on all, and surveillance of each by all, would not grind all down into a tame uniformity of thoughts, feelings, and actions?' (*Political Economy*, II, 1, 3.) Clearly Mill was right in thinking this to be an issue of major importance in deciding for or against socialist and communist social orders. However, his detailed argument is less impressive than the general lines of approach he employed.

Mill argued that we must not judge private property systems simply by how they have worked in the past, for 'the principle of private property has never yet had a fair trial in any country' (*Political Economy*, II, 1, 3). We must compare the ideal of private property with that of socialism. Yet Mill stressed the difficulties in the way of socialism, that it required, in order to work, virtually the moral development of the community, while at the same time neglecting to stress, what he rightly stressed in the discussion of representative government, that the attainability of the ideal is vitally relevant to its relevance. He also here departed from the methodology of the *Logic* to the extent of speaking of and accepting experiments in socialist and private property systems as if they are genuine experiments which bear on the relative superiority of the systems. What here could possibly count as a relevant or decisive experiment? He also argued, seemingly in an *a priori*stic way, that under socialism public opinion would be powerful, and that while this may threaten liberty, it would also bring goods such as easing of overpopulation as a result of censure of sexual intemperance, overpopulation always looming large as an evil for Mill. (Until converted late in life from the Wage Fund Theory by Thornton, Mill thought of overpopulation as the barrier to wage improvements for the workers.) Again, he saw competition, not as the evil which threatens wages, fraternity and co-operation as many socialists have represented it as being, but as useful and desirable, and as a source of initiative, independence, originality and endeavour, although not a security of quality. By contrast, he saw communism and forms of socialism as being faced with problems in securing the required effort and industry from their citizens.

There is, however, much detailed, perceptive comment concerning the evils of his contemporary society, and worthwhile suggestions about improvements. Mill saw that rewards for labour were almost inversely proportional to what was dictated by justice; he noted the difficulty of determining rules of justice here, and expressed support for profit-sharing schemes, co-operatives and the like. That the early hopes about these have not been realised does nothing to make Mill's contribution unimportant. He noted that land was distinct from other forms of property, as being a kind of monopoly; and he was prepared to accept state control of vast companies where individuals cannot effectively compete.

Three important features are missing from Mill's discussions of socialism and communism, the absence of which would surprise a modern socialist. First, there is none of the moral indignation of Marx, Engels, Laski and Tawney at the gross inequalities to be found in capitalist societies; in Mill's writings, there is no deep sense of the workers being shamelessly and unjustly exploited. If the reader looks hard, he can often find calm statements showing awareness that there are serious injustices, but there is no sense of grave moral indignation at the injustices and indignities, the misery and wretchedness, of the victims of the system. Secondly, there is no evident awareness of the power of wealth, of what is true and important in Marxism, that capitalists may use democratic institutions to further their class interests and to oppose reform; that, if constitutional methods fail, resort may be made to violent, unconstitutional methods to oppose change and reform. Thirdly and most important, there is an almost complete unawareness, and certainly, at best, a dismissal without argument, of the argument for socialism from liberty noted in the section on liberty above, that the shortcomings and inequalities of capitalist systems are impediments or obstacles to freedom, and that socialism, by providing employment, reasonable minimum wages, and amenities such as health services, may foster and enlarge liberty. If the main test by which we are to judge between socialism and capitalism is in terms of liberty, this argument concerning liberty is of vital importance. It may be, as many contemporary Millians have argued, that it rests on a mistaken concept of liberty. I suggest that this is not so, but this needs to be argued. Further, Mill seems to have failed to appreciate the importance of many goods other than liberty, which are threatened by an uncontrolled competitive economic system. It is not simply liberty that is threatened. Goods such as human happiness, access for the talented to higher education and culture, indeed even to education, and to those many things stressed in *Liberty*, including rational, lively, true belief, may be

140

threatened or lost. The solution may well be one which Mill, if he lived today, would have favoured, namely, a compromise between socialism and a private property system, a controlled competitive system of the kind found in the modern welfare state. Mill, in his writings on socialism, communism and private property systems, was never doctrinaire. He approached each on the basis of their determinable merits. Hence it is not improbable that something along the lines of a less centralised welfare state may have been accepted by him as the most satisfactory compromise in the modern, tightly interdependent world situation.

5 Metaphysics: The Nature of Reality

Mill nowhere set out a systematic statement of his metaphysical theories. However, his *An Examination of Sir William Hamilton's Philosophy* contains discussions of problems in metaphysics, philosophical psychology and logic. It is predominantly expository and polemical in character, Mill's main concern being to expose the inadequacies of Hamilton's, Mansel's and others' arguments and theories; he advanced his own theories as more satisfactory alternatives, but without detailed development. Although most English-speaking philosophers have some (usually indirect) acquaintance with this work, it is one of limited importance. Mill discussed metaphysical issues in other writings, including the *Logic, Theism* and *Berkeley's Life and Writings*.

Mill's treatment of the problem of universals and of causality has been noted in Chapter 2; his contributions to the philosophy of religion will be discussed in Chapter 6. Here it is metaphysics as relating to the nature of the external world, matter and mind, that will be considered. Mill's view was that all reality is mental, that matter and material objects, if conceived of as things distinct from mental phenomena, were philosophers' and theologians' illusions, the belief in which could be explained in terms of the psychological tendency to 'mistake mental abstractions, even negative ones, for substantive realities'. The sources of his inspiration were Hartley's *Observations on Man* (1749) which set out the Associationist psychology, and Berkeley's idealist writings. Mill indicated his estimates of the importance of Berkeley and Hartley in the history of philosophy when he wrote that of 'all who, from the earliest times, have applied the powers of their minds to

142

metaphysical inquiries, he [Berkeley] is the one of greatest philosophic genius: though among these are included Plato, Hobbes, Locke, Hartley, and Hume; Descartes, Spinoza, Leibnitz, and Kant' ('Berkeley's Life and Writings', in *Fortnightly Review*, 1 Nov 1871, p. 505). Mill was also indebted to his father and to A. Bain. Thus his writings here lack any claim to significant originality, as he simply expressed the phenomenalist element which can be separated from Berkeley's theistic idealism in a slogan form which has since caught on, that 'Matter is a permanent possibility of sensation'.

The Nature of the External World

The commonsense view is that the things we perceive, chairs, tables, houses, cars, other people, are real and external to us, and not dependent on us for their existence, and that our knowledge of them springs from our sense perceptions. We see, touch, feel, hear or taste them. There are obvious grounds for questioning these commonsense beliefs. Our senses may mislead us, such that things cannot always be as they appear; the straight stick, in water, appears bent, parallel lines appear to meet in the distance, we see mirages, people experience hallucinations. Further, science suggests that the colour and other features of objects are not qualities inherent in the things perceived but the results of interactions between things and observers. There would therefore seem to be a real problem concerning the nature and our knowledge of the external world. Yet this is not quite how the problem arose for Mill. His approach consisted rather in examining the origins of our beliefs, and what is necessary to explain them.

Mill rejected the realist theory that we directly intuit material objects, and the more qualified view of Hamilton, that we know directly the so-called primary qualities (extension, solidity, figure, etc.). His grounds were various. Part of his case for rejecting direct realism of any kind consisted in his detailed account of how we come to gain knowledge of the qualities of objects. *Hamilton*, chap. 13, contains a careful, detailed discussion of the origin and basis of our belief in the primary qualities. Equally important is the claim that 'it is impossible to doubt a fact of internal consciousness', that 'to feel, and not to know that we feel is an impossibility' (ibid., p. 163), and that we can fully explain our belief in the external world by reference to these indubitable sense experiences (sensations) and the laws of the mind. There is no systematic exploration of the direct realist contention that we have direct awareness of the real world (illusory perceptions can be explained as errors, and much done to render the theory more plausible than Mill represented it as being), and similarly, while Mill noted and commented on a number of causal theories such as the representative theory of perception, Kantian phenomena–noumena theories (if they can accurately be characterised as causal theories), he engaged in no systematic examination of them, instead resting his rejection of them on two main considerations, namely, that it is possible to explain the external world without reference to these unknowable causes of sensations, and that on a correct understanding of causality there can be no grounds for postulating such unknowable causes.

Mill sought to explain the belief in the external world in terms of sensations, possible sensations and psychological laws, including the law that we are capable of expectation (and memory) of possible (actual) sensations, and the various laws of association that 'similar phenomena tend to be thought together', 'Phenomena which have either been experienced or conceived in close contiguity to one another, tend to be thought together – the kinds of contiguity being simultaneity and immediate succession', 'Associations produced by contiguity become more certain and rapid by repetition, this leading to inseparable and indissoluble association', Mill here observing that when an association acquires this character of inseparability, the facts or phenomena answering to those ideas come at last to seem inseparable in existence; 'things we are unable to conceive apart appear incapable of existing apart'. Mill therefore stated the Psychological Theory which he explained as maintaining 'that there are associations naturally and even necessarily generated by the order of our sensations and of our reminiscences of sensation, which, supposing no intuition of the external world to have existed in consciousness, would inevitably generate the belief, and cause it to be regarded as an intuition' (ibid., p. 227). In this way Mill sought to show that all that is meant by 'material object' (matter) can be explained in terms of actual or possible sensations, that there is no need to postulate anything over and above sensations and possible sensations, ordered and grouped in certain ways, to explain what ordinary people and philosophers mean when they speak of material objects. Mill's so-called Psychological Theory is now seen as one of the early statements of Phenomenalism. His more detailed statement runs:

I see a piece of white paper on a table. I go into another room. If the phaenonenom always followed me, or if, when it did not follow me, I believed it to disappear *è rerum naturâ*, I should not believe it to be an external object. I should consider it as a phantom – a mere affection of my senses. ... But, though I have ceased to see it, I am persuaded that the paper is still there. ... I believe that when I again place myself in the circumstances in which I had those sensations, that is, when I go again into the room, I shall again have them; and further, that there has been no intervening moment at which this would not have been the case. Owing to this property of my mind, my conception of the world at any instant consists, in only a small proportion, of present sensations. ... The conception I form of the world existing at any moment, comprises, along with the sensations I am feeling, a countless variety of possibilities of sensation: namely, the whole of those which past observation tells me that I could, under any supposable circumstances, experience at this moment, together with an indefinite and illimitable multitude of others which though I do not know that I could, yet it is possible that I might, experience in circumstances not known to me. These various possibilities are the important thing to me in the world. My present sensations are generally of little importance, and are moreover fugitive: the possibilities, on the contrary, are permanent, which is the character which mainly distinguishes our idea of Substance or Matter from our notion of sensation. These possibilities, which are conditional certainties, need a special name to distinguish them from mere vague possibilities, which experience gives no warrant for reckoning upon. (ibid., pp. 228–9)

Matter, then, may be defined, a Permanent Possibility of Sensation.... But I affirm with confidence, that this conception of matter includes the whole meaning attached to it by the common world, apart from philosophical and sometimes from theological, theories. The reliance of mankind on the real existence of visible and tangible objects, means reliance on the reality and permanence of Possibilities of visual and tactual sensations, when no such sensations are actually experienced. (ibid., p. 233)

Mill claimed that his account covered belief in primary qualities as successfully as it did belief concerning secondary qualities, in chap. 13 entering into a lengthy discussion of primary qualities, and arguing that resistance, extension, touch, are to be explained in terms of muscular movement. Thus, on Mill's account, when we believe in the existence of material objects, what we believe in are actual and possible sensations, or simply possible sensations, where the sensations are thought of as coming in groups, in such a way that, as a result of association of ideas, some are symbols or signs of others. Thus, when we observe a horse, i.e. have visual horse-type sensations, we, in believing it to be a real horse, a material object, believe that we should experience the other material object horse sensations if we touched, felt, smelt it. This Mill expressed by saying that some possibilities are conditional certainties and, less accurately, that they are permanent possibilities, and potentialities. In asserting that material objects exist, for example that there is a cat in the next room, I am concerned to assert the existence of things which have *public, independent* and, in some sense, *continuing* existence, where the contrast is with purely private sensations such as a pain, hallucination, sensations as of mirages (which may be shared but not be independent of observers), purely imagined objects, and mere fleeting phenomena such as a flash of lightning. In believing the cat to be a material object, we believe that it is public, observable in principle, and usually in practice, by other observers; that its existence is independent of our perceptions, such that it continues to exist (unless changed or destroyed) when not observed; and that its existence is a continuing one in that it has temporal duration. Mill sought to accommodate these features in his slogan statement 'Matter is a permanent possibility of sensation'.

Even though this statement is often quoted with approval, it is an inaccurate, misleading summary of Mill's thesis. Mill used it to express a number of claims. He wished to note the enduring connections between the sensations within each group of material object sensations, stones, horses, trees, by explaining the possibility of experiencing some after experiencing other of the sensations as *permanent*. This is an intelligible but less illuminating description than other possible ones: it is the connection between the actual and the possible, or some and other possible sensations, rather than the possibilities, which are permanent. Mill also wished to note that objects, e.g. prehistoric plants and animals, may exist independently of all observation. Mill's summary statement explains their existence as of there being permanent, indefinitely lasting possibilities of sensations of these now non-existent entities. Here he seems to use 'permanent' in its ordinary sense. He also sought to explain the continuing existence of things after we cease to observe them. This we often express by observing that while the table is permanent, our perceptions of it are not. This too he sought to note by speaking of the possibilities as permanent. In fact, material objects are not permanent in the sense of lasting indefinitely; hence the possibilities of observing them, e.g. by re-entering the room, ought to be no more permanent than the material objects the belief in the existence of which is being explained. It could be argued that 'permanent' has a legitimate use in all these contexts, namely, that all the so-called permanent possibilities, if expressed in terms of hypothetical propositions, claim permanent truth. Thus it is claimed to be permanently true that some sensations are signs of others, e.g. that certain this-horse sensations are signs of other this-horse sensations; that sensations consequent on change of the observer's position would/will occur; that had an observer been present (none could be), certain sensations would have been experienced. Mill did seem to view these as permanent hypothetical truths, but this sense of 'permanent' would not exhaust his meaning or be adequate for the purpose of his theory. Further, the first hypothetical is not a permanent truth; deception, where some sensations are wrongly taken as signs of others, occurs. More will be said concerning these issues later; here, what is important is that Mill attempted to express in summary form what can only accurately be expressed in longer, more qualified statements.

Mill's account of matter is a reductionist one. He sought to explain the world in terms of sensations, certain orders or arrangements of sensations and possible sensations, without reference to matter, substance, qualities. However, he neither represented not advanced it as such, but rather as a translation of ordinary material object statements. He claimed simply to explain what we mean by matter, that we assert no more than a permanent possibility of sensations when we assert that matter exists. (He did concede that some philosophers and theologians invoked some other concept or concepts of matter, and he noted the strength of the human tendency to mistake mental

148

abstractions for substantive realities; hence he did not completely rule out the reductionist aspect of his account.)

Mill's account may now best be further explained and examined by considering objections which have been pressed against it, and against a modern type of restatement of phenomenalism in terms of hypothetical propositions. What Mill expressed in terms of possibilities may be restated in terms of sets of hypothetical propositions of a complex character. Thus, 'There is a cat on the chair before me' means 'I have cat–chair type visual sensations, and if I move and touch (them), I will have fur and wood type sensations, etc., and if other observers enter the room and look in that direction they will experience one or other of a number of disjunctive sets of sensations of shape, colour, size, etc.' 'There is a cat in the next room' will mean 'If I or any other observer enters the next room and looks in the appropriate direction, I or he will experience sets of sensations (not necessarily the same set but from a range of sets) of the chair–cat groups.' And 'Dinosaurs existed in prehistoric Siberia' (hereafter it will be convenient to assume that they never co-existed with man) means 'If there had been observers, and if they had been in Siberia, and had looked in the appropriate direction at the right time, they would have experienced one or other of a range of sets of sensations which we now characterise as sensations of a dinosaur.' These of course are only suggested beginnings of such translations. A common objection to phenomenalism, and to Mill's account in particular, is that phenomenalists have failed to carry out the translation of material object statements into sensation (sense data) statements. Mill, for example, invoked material object expressions to explain his analysis, even though it was designed to replace such expressions. Consider the following proposed translation:

I believe that Calcutta exists, though I do not perceive it, and that it would still exist if every percipient inhabitant were suddenly to leave the place, or be struck dead. But when I analyse the belief, all I find in it is, that were these events to take place, the Permanent Possibility of Sensation which I call Calcutta would still remain; that if I were suddenly transported to the banks of the Hoogly, I should still have the sensations which, if now present, would lead me to affirm that Calcutta exists here and now. (ibid., p. 235)

... the very idea of anything out of ourselves is derived solely from the knowledge experience gives us of the Permanent Possibilities. Our sensations we carry with us wherever we go, and they never exist where we are not; but when we change our place we do not carry away with us the Permanent Possibility of sensation: they remain until we return. (ibid., p. 238)

And when analysed to the bottom on the principles of the Associative Psychology, the brain, just as much as the mental functions is, like matter itself, merely a set of human sensations either actual or inferred as possible, namely those which the anatomist has when he opens the skull, and the impressions which we suppose we should receive of molecular or some other movements when the cerebral action was going on, if there were no bony envelope and our senses or our instruments were sufficiently delicate.
(*Theism*, 1st ed., pp. 199–200; Toronto and R.K.P. ed., pp. 461–2)

We find other people grounding their expectations and conduct upon the same permanent possibilities on which we ground ours. But we do not find them experiencing the same actual sensations. Other people do not have our sensations exactly when and as we have them: but they have our possibilities of sensation; whatever indicates a present possibility of sensations to ourselves, indicates a present possibility of similar sensations to them, except so far as their organs of sensations may vary from the type of ours. (*Hamilton*, p. 232)

150

In an Appendix to chaps 11 and 12, Mill dismissed the criticism about translation as trivial, arguing that there is no difficulty in principle in making the translation in full, and that it is as a matter of expository convenience that he continued to use material object language (see esp. p. 251). Others have suggested that the difficulty in completing the translation springs simply from the poverty of language, that to approach giving a complete translation would involve much linguistic inventiveness. None the less a careful consideration of the first three of the above statements of Mill suggests that the failure to complete the translations is due to the inadequacy of the theory. All involve reference to physical movement to take note in the translations of the notions of physical and temporal location. To complete these translations, the references to the observer, his position, and his sense organs must be replaced by sensation statements, and the completed translation of the Calcutta statement would run something like: 'If sensations of travelling to and looking at Calcutta and the Hoogly are experienced, some of the group of Calcutta and Hoogly sensations will be experienced (if experienced, i.e. if the sense organs are normal), and other Calcutta and Hoogly sensations will be experienced if sensations as of moving around Calcutta or of entering the Hoogly are experienced, provided that the sensations of light, etc., are also in the former case experienced.' Berlin's point, that hypotheticals can be true and yet nothing exist, is relevant, for on this fuller, more complete translation the assertion can be true and yet nothing, not even sensations, exist. Even with this translation there are evident difficulties in translating out the reference to normal sense organs. If there had never been and never were sensations as of an observer travelling to and positioning himself to observe Calcutta on the Hoogly, i.e. if the antecedent clause were never fulfilled, the assertion would still be true if the consequent were/would be consequent on the truth of the antecedent. This is not so with genuine material object statements. For them to be true, something must exist. The analysis further implies that all logically possible material objects exist. This suggests that the analysis must be restated in terms of actual possibilities, and not simply possibilities, yet this too leads to difficulties, as with prehistoric phenomena.

This attempt to complete the translations shows that Mill's statement that 'though the sensations cease, the possibilities remain in existence; they are independent of our will, our presence, and everything which belongs to us' is not due to careless writing but a statement of an implication of his theory: for Mill, possibilities must exist even in the absence of sensations (and hence sensors); possible sensations are, for him, realities of some sort. We ordinarily accept as significant, talk about possible sensations because we think of actual or possible sensors. If the example, by definition, excludes such possible sensors, it would seem thereby to make inapplicable and meaningless talk about possible sensations. This is denied in Mill's account. The importance of this difficulty becomes evident when other difficulties are examined.

The translation of the last passage above involves problems concerning the nature and existence of other human bodies and human persons. 'Bertrand Russell exists' would, on this analysis, be translated into the permanent possibility of Bertrand Russellish sensations. Human bodies and human persons will be analysed into certain types of sensations, actual and possible, the former like other material object sensation translations such as those relating to horses, apes, and the latter including reference to 'talk' and 'response' types of sensations. However, there are no grounds for attributing to these sensations, and not to horse and ape sensations, separate existence, independently of us. Mill suggested that we infer, using an argument by analogy (according to the *Logic* an unreliable mode of argument although useful as a source of hypotheses), that these person types of groups of sensations have sensations like our sensations. Seeking to show that he was not committed to solipsism, Mill here argued:

All that I am compelled to admit if I receive this theory, is that other people's Selves also are but series of feelings, like my own. Though my Mind, as I am capable of conceiving it, be nothing but the succession of my feelings, and though Mind itself may be merely a possibility of feelings, there is nothing in that doctrine to prevent my conceiving, and believing, that there are other successions of feelings besides those of which I am conscious, and that these are as real as my own.... By what evidence do I know ... that there exist other sentient creatures; that the walking and speaking figures which I see and hear, have sensations and thoughts, or in other words, possess Minds? ... I conclude it from certain things, which my experience of my own states proves to me to be marks of it. ... I conclude that other human beings have feelings like me, because, first, they have bodies like me, which I know, in my own case, to be the antecedent condition of feelings; and because, secondly, they exhibit the acts, and other outward signs, which in my own case I know by experience to be caused by feelings. I am conscious in myself of a series of facts connected by a uniform sequence, of which the beginning is modifications of my body, the middle is feelings, and the end is outward demeanour. In the case of other human beings I have the evidence of my senses for the first and last links of the series, but not for the intermediate link. I find, however, that the sequence between the first and last is as regular and constant in those other cases as it is in mine. In my own case I know that the first link produces the last through the intermediate link, and could not produce it without. Experience, therefore, obliges me to conclude that there must be an intermediate link; which must either be the same in others as in myself, or a different one: I must either be the same in others as in myself, or a different one. I must either believe them to be alive or to be automatons ... and by believing them to be alive ... I bring other human beings, as phaenomena under the same generalisations which I know by experience to be the true theory of my own existence. And in doing so I conform to the legitimate rules of experimental inquiry. The process is exactly parallel to that by which Newton proved that the force which keeps the planets in their orbits is identical with that by which an apple falls to the ground.... We know the existence of other beings by generalisation from the knowledge of our own.... This logical process loses none of its legitimacy on the supposition that neither Mind nor Matter is anything but a permanent possibility of feeling.... I look about me, and though there is only one group (or body) which is connected with all my sensations in this peculiar manner, I observe that there is a great multitude of other bodies, closely resembling in their sensible properties (...) this particular one, whose modifications do not call up, as those of my own body do, a world of sensations in my consciousness. Since they do not do so in my consciousness, I infer that they do it out of my consciousness, and that to each of them belongs a world of consciousness of its own, to which it stands in the same relation in which what I call my body stands to mine. (ibid., pp. 242–5)

The existence of other minds constitutes a problem for most theories. Mill was right to insist that even the most extreme Intuitionist is unprepared to claim direct awareness of other minds (persons). Most theorists invoke some such argument by analogy as Mill's and reinforce it by appeal to facts about communication, etc. Hence, Mill might seem to be no less satisfactorily placed here than other theorists. This is not so, for the carrying through of the phenomenalist translation destroys the basis on which the argument by analogy rests. No doubt other arguments can be devised, but this is the argument advanced by Mill.

This difficulty concerning the existence of other people as simply peculiar sensations of our own, which emerges from an attempt to complete the translation, leads to the further consequence that the suggestion, that in explaining the possibilities/hypotheticals

154

which constitute elements in the translation, we must include reference to possible sensations of actual and possible people, is ill based. This is of importance in respect of unobservable and unobserved objects, for example prehistoric plants and animals. Consider the statement above from *Hamilton*, p. 232.

The expression 'permanent' (and its counterparts in the hypothetical version of phenomenalism) also gives rise to difficulties. Mill used this expression to note various different things: the groupings of material object sensations, the public, independent character of material objects, and the existence of unobserved and unobservable objects. It serves its purpose in respect of unobserved objects only at the cost of difficulties with secondary qualities. (Mill on p. 239 of *Hamilton* acknowledged that secondary qualities vary from person to person and may vary with the one person from time to time, such that the one object may, on this view, be a number of ranges of distinct actual and/or possible sensations of each kind.) Further, it complicates and renders less plausible Mill's account of unstable, changing material objects. When we assert of ice standing in the sun, the log on the fire, the bomb whose fuse has been triggered, that they are material objects, we do not assert that they give rise to permanent possibilities of sensation in any ordinary sense of that expression. Mill seemed to acknowledge this when he discussed the ice and the log, arguing that: 'Changes in the Permanent Possibilities I find to have always for their antecedent conditions, other Permanent Possibilities, and to be connected with them by an order or law, as uniform as that which connects the elements of each group with one another; indeed by a still stricter order, for the laws of succession, those of Cause and Effect, are laws of more rigid precision than those of simultaneousness' (ibid., p. 257). Mill's move here copes with the changing objects he cited, but at the expense of difficulty concerning prehistoric objects. For them to have had existence, the permanent possibilities of certain, now extinct, fern and dinosaur sensations must still exist. Yet on Mill's account of the permanent possibilities of the log and ice sensations, the fernish and dinosaurish permanent possibilities are no more. If that is so, and it is relevant that the fern and dinosaur ceased to exist as a result of the operation of causal laws, then on this account they could never have existed. Further, when it is claimed that an object is real, we make no claim about its continued existence, nor are we committed to any view about its changing in accord with knowable laws of nature. Whatever may be the merits of Hume's and Mill's accounts of miracles, we are not, by virtue of the logic of material object discourse, committed to denying that a miraculous disappearance of a material object, e.g. an orange, may occur, when we assert that it is a material object. Hence in the ordinary sense and in that which Mill used above of 'permanent', a claim that matter, i.e. that a material object, exists, need not involve any claim to conditional permanence of the possibilities of sensations. The version of phenomenalism in terms of hypothetical propositions is less obviously but none the less equally exposed to this criticism. When I assert that there is a block of ice in the next room, I do not assert, and would be misunderstood if believed to be asserting, that if any observer in the future entered the room he would have ice-group type sensations (unless the ice had melted). This might be a reasonable assumption to make, but it is not the essential meaning of my assertion. Further, the meaning or correct translations of material object statements do not vary according to whether one believes in universal causality, whether the object is incapable of change or subject to change, but according to unknown laws or in a lawless way.

The fact of change, together with the need to acknowledge the existence of material objects prior to the existence of sensory beings, makes it vital for the phenomenalist to introduce reference to temporal as well as spatial location in the translations he offers. Mill could have explained the burning log or the melting ice by saying that the possibilities were existent at times '*t to t*'. Thus it has been argued that if someone had observed the world in prehistoric time T, at the right place, etc., he would have had dinosaur-group type sensations. This move encounters its own difficulties, first that of explaining time. Mill noted this problem and sought to explain time in terms of successions of sensations (see *Hamilton*, p. 253). On such an account of time, the account of prehistory would involve reference to hypothetical sensations and hypothetical succession between these sensations. If there were no observers, i.e. all human beings had died, it is hard to make sense of these hypotheticals; yet in asserting that prehistoric plants existed, we are asserting that they existed, no matter what happens to the human race. Further, this whole account involves the treating of possibilities as actualities of some sort. If and in so far as it is asserted that the object which no longer exists is still in some sense a permanent possibility of sensation, and also that objects such as the earth will continue to exist after the last human being dies, in the sense of being a continuing permanent possibility of sensation, it is being claimed that the possibilities will exist and have temporal location without sensors and successions of sensations.

Mind

Mill sought to explain mind as well as matter in terms of permanent possibilities. His account ran thus:

> We have no conception of Mind itself, as distinguished from its conscious manifestations. We neither know nor can imagine it, except as represented by the succession of manifold feelings which metaphysicians call by the name of States or modifications of mind. ... The belief I entertain that my mind exists when it is not feeling, nor thinking, nor conscious of its own existence, resolves itself into the belief of a Permanent Possibility of these States. (ibid., p. 241)

The sense in which Mill used 'permanent' here is not clear. The permanent possibilities of experiencing mental states cannot easily be explained as a permanent hypothetical truth of some sort, for while the nature of the consequent is clear, it is not clear how the antecedent is meaningfully to be filled in. Mill introduced the reference to permanence to explain the continuing existence ascribed to the self or mind when asleep or unconscious; the mind is thought to exist both when experiencing sensations and thoughts and as long as the possibility of its doing so continues. (The assertion that a mind exists claims more than simply that there can be sensations here and now.) However, this is distinct from its being a permanent, i.e. indefinitely lasting, possibility of experiencing these states. In ascribing minds to ourselves we are not claiming the immortality to which a literal interpretation of Mill's account would seem to commit us. At most, Mill ought to have argued that the mind exists while there is a continuing possibility of these states. Even then, his account would not be an accurate statement of what the ordinary man means by a mind (or a person, persons being mind-complexes of a certain kind for Mill), for the ordinary person thinks that minds, persons, may continue to exist even after any real possibility of such mental experiences ceases, for example where there is severe brain damage.

So too it may be asked, what it is that possesses these possibilities. One cannot have possibilities of mental sensations existing in the absence of all else; the apparent sense of the statement rests on the unspoken assumption that the possibilities are some sort of dispositional property of the mind. Eliminate all reference to a mind, distinct from mental states, and the allusion to permanent possibilities ceases to have plausibility, indeed meaning. Yet in suggesting this account, Mill was seeking to explain mind entirely in terms of *its* actual and possible states. A full translation would require the reference to *its*, the *mind's*, states to be written out of the translation.

Mill expressed uneasiness concerning such an

account, and concluded his discussion with an unsatisfactory paradox, but no coherent account of mind. In his later *Berkeley's Life and Writings* he wrote, perhaps significantly, of the existence of minds and their states. He was uneasy in *Hamilton* because his account involved memory and expectation, yet these involve, unlike a sensation, more than simply a present existence. Memory involves a present mental state relating to a past experience or sensation, and expectation an anticipation of a future sensation. Further, they suggest, as Mill acknowledged, self-awareness and self-identity, i.e. a belief in the self-sameness of the series. The account of mind in terms of actual and possible mental states is incapable of accommodating such facts. This led Mill to indicate the paradox and hopefully, but strangely for such a rationalist and empiricist, to enjoin the acceptance of Mind as an inexplicable, i.e. a Mystery. Mill here wrote:

The fact believed is, that the sensations did actually form, or will hereafter form, part of the self-same series of states, or thread of consciousness, of which the remembrance or expectation of those sensations is the part now present. If, therefore, we speak of the Mind as a series of feelings, we are obliged to complete the statement by calling it a series of feelings which is aware of itself as past and future: and we are reduced to the alternative of believing that Mind, or Ego, is something different from any series of feelings, or possibilities of them, or of accepting the paradox, that something which *ex hypothesi* is but a series of feelings, can be aware of itself as a series.

The truth is, that we are here face to face with that final inexplicability, at which, as Sir W. Hamilton observes, we inevitably arrive when we reach ultimate facts; and in general, one mode of stating it only appears more incomprehensible than another, because the whole of human language is accommodated to the one, and is so incongruous with the other, that it cannot be expressed in any terms which do not deny its truth. The real stumbling block is perhaps not in any theory of the fact, but in the fact itself. The true incomprehensibility perhaps is, that something which has ceased, or is not yet in existence, can still be, in a manner, present: that a series of feelings, the infinitely greater part of which is past or future, can be gathered up, as it were, into a single present conception, accompanied by a belief of reality. I think, by far the wisest thing we can do, is to accept the inexplicable fact, without any theory of how it takes place; and when we are obliged to speak of it in terms which assume a theory, to use them with a reservation as to their meaning. (*Hamilton*, p. 248)

6 Philosophy of Religion

Mill did not develop a systematic, detailed philosophy of religion, but rather made brief excursions into that territory. His main contributions are to be found in *Three Essays on Religion*, published in 1874 by Helen Taylor, *An Examination of Sir William Hamilton's Philosophy*, especially chap. 7, and *Auguste Comte and Positivism*. Two of the three essays, *On Nature* and *The Utility of Religion*, were written between 1850 and 1858, and the third essay, *Theism*, between 1868 and 1870. The essay *Nature* is something of a miscellany, and includes a range of comments on the concepts nature, natural, and on ethics and religion. The other two essays are also of a discursive character, and are often superficial. There are significant differences in both the tone and the detailed conclusions of the earlier and later essays. This might reasonably have been expected. What is unexpected is the character of the differences. The earlier writings are unsympathetic to religion; *Theism* is sympathetic and verges on the tendentious in its arriving at a theistic conclusion. In the earlier essays there is full awareness of the fact of evil, and some sympathy with a Manichaean position, that there is a contriving goodness and a principle of evil, as one view compatible with the known facts. In *Theism*, Mill used a very strained argument in support of a monotheistic position, that there is a finite contriving goodness, i.e. a benevolent good god who, although not the creator of the world, brings about the changes and order in the world. This goes with a playing down of the enormity of evil, so much so that, had Mill seriously brought together the discussions of evil in the earlier essays and his argument for the benevolence of his god in *Theism*, his conclusion in the latter would necessarily have had to be modified.

The argument for religion from its alleged utility has come in many forms. It has been argued that religion is useful as a cohesive factor, holding society and society's morality together in such a way that he who attacks society's religion attacks society. Religion has also been commended as a source of strength and consolation. More importantly, it is argued that religion is useful and even essential for moral education, moral endeavour and moral achievement, this contention surviving the general Protestant abandonment and Roman Catholic playing down of the doctrines of heaven and hell with which it was formerly usually associated. Mill's major concern is with this third type of contention, although his discussion is relevant to all three. Mill's opening objection to this whole approach is that, if religion is true, it is useful. As noted in chap. 4, this is not necessarily so: true beliefs may be harmful, false beliefs useful; hence Mill was mistaken in suggesting that the need to argue for the utility of religion arises from lack of conviction of its truth. It may, but need not, spring from such doubts. Mill's moral objection is a more serious one, but resting as it does on a valuation of integrity and honesty for their own sakes, it is one which is not available to him as a hedonistic utilitarianism, and is in any case relevant only against those who commend religion whether or not it be true. Mill argued that the appeal to the utility of religion is 'an appeal to unbelievers, to induce them to practise a well-meant hypocrisy, or to semi-believers to make them avert their eyes from what might possibly shake their unstable belief, or finally to persons in general to abstain from expressing any doubts they may feel, since a fabric of immense importance to mankind is so insecure at its foundations, that men must hold their breath in its neighbourhood for fear of blowing it down' (*Three Essays on Religion*, 1st ed., p. 70; Toronto and R.K.P. ed., p. 403).

In his subsequent discussion, Mill separated the question 'Is religion vital to the temporal welfare of mankind?' from that concerning the utility of particular religions. Many religions have brought great harm to mankind; here, Mill's very favourable assessment of Christianity and of Christ are surprising in the light on the one hand of his utilitarianism and on the other of the ethical theories of Plato and Aristotle. Mill argued that in the moral sphere the utility of religion has been overstated, that it is authority, e.g. the State, education and public opinion, which are efficacious in bringing about conformity with desired moral standards; that it is only because religion is often associated with these factors that it appears to have the utility it does. Mill noted the lack of efficacy of postponed, indefinite rewards and punishments; he also noted Bentham's arguments, Bentham having noted the lack of correlation between the religious condemnation and respect for moral injunctions such as those relating to the taking of oaths, duelling and 'illicit sexual intercourse', the latter being claimed by the religious to be equally wrong for the male and female, but more commonly engaged in by the male because less severely censured by public opinion.

Mill's comments on the efficacy of early education, pressure from public opinion and the State appear to be correct, but his apparent acceptance of these means of achieving moral conformity ill accord with the liberal permissiveness of *Liberty*; yet he seemed not simply to be offering *ad hominem* arguments, although the terms of the argument are based on the premiss that moral conformity is desirable, and the issue that concerning whether religion is useful in achieving this end. As elsewhere, Mill made no attempt to reach his conclusion by using his concrete and inverse deductive methods of discovery and proof.

Mill conceded some value to religious belief, in that, like poetry, it satisfies the want 'of ideal conceptions grander and more beautiful than we see realized in the prose of human life' (ibid., 1st ed., p. 103; Toronto and R.K.P. ed., p. 419). And as against Comte's religion of humanity, he noted that the more orthodox religious belief in immortality might seem to be an advantage.

At the same time he noted that many have done very well without such a belief, and were he writing today, he would have been more conscious of how loosely connected the two beliefs are. In any case, whether or not a belief in personal immortality is 'advantageous' depends very much on the person and on his other beliefs; the thought of endless existence is distressing rather than comforting to many of the more thoughtful. It would have been interesting to have had Mill's comments on Marx's assessment of religion as part of the superstructure and hence a means of class oppression. No doubt he would have rejected this assessment, but it might have made him appreciate the need for a much more searching, scientific and less impressionistic approach to the question.

The Existence of God

Mill briefly examined some of the more common and popular arguments for the existence of God, and rather more fully those from miracles and design. His mode of argument consisted in rejecting at the outset all *a priori* arguments from ideas or convictions in our minds, and instead testing the arguments against the facts revealed by experience. This limits the value of his discussion, as many who advance such arguments would reject this whole approach. Thus, while Mill makes some useful comments concerning the argument from first cause and the ontological argument, his discussions would be dismissed by exponents of these arguments as not touching on the crucial issues. His comments concerning the argument from the general consent of mankind, and Kant's argument to God's existence from our apprehension of duty, are more relevant and effective, pointing out as they do the inadequacy of the grounds upon which these arguments are based.

Mill here asked: 'Can any evidence suffice to prove a Divine Revelation? And of what nature and amount must that evidence be?' (*Theism*, ibid., 1st ed., p. 215; Toronto and R.K.P. ed., p. 469.) He rejected internal revelations, claiming that they could be self-authenticating only in respect of their moral character, and that the best conceivable moral revelation would be inadequate to sustain the authenticity of the revelation. Thus he went on to argue: 'A Revelation therefore, cannot be proved divine unless by external evidence; that is, by the exhibition of supernatural facts. And we have to consider, whether it is possible to prove supernatural facts, and if it is, what evidence is required to prove them' (ibid., 1st ed., pp. 216–17; Toronto and R.K.P. ed., p. 470). The most obvious, apparent cases of external revelation are miracles. Here Mill approached the question via Hume's celebrated discussion. (In the *Logic*, III, 25, 2, the problem arose in respect of induction, in *Theism* it is in respect of the proof of God's existence.) In the latter Mill asked: What would count as evidence for a miracle (i.e. a marvellous event due to some supernatural cause and contrary to the laws of nature)? Can there now be evidence which would be adequate to establish that a miracle has occurred? Could there be adequate evidence of the occurrence of miracles, if there are independent reasons for believing in the existence of a supernatural being? Although Mill argued: 'It is evidently impossible to maintain that if a supernatural fact really occurs, proof of its occurrence cannot be accessible to human faculties. The evidence of our senses could prove this as it can prove other things' (ibid., 1st ed., p. 217; Toronto and R.K.P. ed., p. 470); and, although he cited as an illustration of what would count as a series of well-authenticated miracles (the seeing of a being – an invisible, supernatural being? – bring new worlds into being), Mill in fact ended by arguing that now (1870), in the present stage in the development of science, no imaginable evidence could be adequate to sustain a belief that a miracle had occurred, and that the alternative hypotheses will always be more probable, an inference being involved in each case. The alternative hypotheses are that the testimony is mistaken, false, etc., or that the phenomenon is to be explained in terms of at present unknown, more remote laws of nature. Thus Mill was committed by his arguments to the strangely paradoxical conclusion that there may well be miraculous events, and that we shall never have adequate grounds for accepting them as such. The crux of his argument is that the law-governed character of the universe is now established. The obvious reply is that evident in chap. 2, that the law-governed character of the universe is to be established only by establishing the causal principle as a synthetic *a priori* principle; that Mill denied that it was such but failed to offer good reasons for believing in the universality of causality. Our knowledge of causal laws is very limited, and while we are in ignorance of so many laws, and even whether there are laws governing all phenomena, the most that can be claimed is that there is a probability that the universe is completely law-governed, such that every event, every phenomenon, is a result of the operation of some causal law. At best the probability need not be a high one. This was seen in the discussion of Mill's attempt to justify the causal principle by induction by simple enumeration. There he acknowledged that we are entitled to accept it as holding only within the limits of human experience, and not in the remoter parts of the universe. Further, as Mill's early observation noted, there would be something fundamentally unsatisfactory with an inductive logic which involved false conclusions being accepted in this way, i.e. that if real miracles occurred and were reliably witnessed and well authenticated, they were always to be rejected as not real miracles.

A probability calculus such as that indicated by Mill is obviously suspect if it makes to be improbable and contrary to the weight of evidence (whatever the evidence) that non-law-like events occur, whether or not such events do occur. Even today it is not out of the question that phenomena occur which are counter to all causal laws. It is easy to imagine the sorts of investigations which might be entered into and which would justify the conclusion that some phenomena are not subject to natural causal laws, and hence are without causes or are products of supernatural causes. However, it is hard to see what added evidence could bear on deciding whether the phenomena had no cause or were products of supernatural causes. This fact alone would make any attempt to prove the existence of God from a miraculous occurrence unsuccessful unless it could be established that the causal principle was a synthetic *a priori* truth; and even then, the objection that no miraculous occurrence could be sufficiently wonderful to provide grounds for calling its cause God would be fatal to the claim.

Mill's discussion of the evidence for miracles, where there are independent grounds for believing in the existence of God, is equally unsatisfactory. He claimed that even here the evidence must be rejected as inadequate, arguing from our knowledge of God's mode of governing the world, namely, that God governs the world through general laws. This is what is in dispute between Mill and the theist; hence Mill's argument here is a simple *petitio principii*.

The Argument from Design

Although in *Hamilton*, chap. 12, Mill interpreted the argument from design as an argument by analogy, in *Theism* he claimed it to be much more and better than this, being a strict inductive argument based on the method of agreement. That method, it will be recalled, is that of looking for instances and antecedents of a phenomenon, and is symbolised: $ABC - abc, ADE - ade; A - a$. Mill, in a strange argument, saw in the complex adaptation of the parts of the eye to its function of seeing, evidence of an intelligent designer (ibid., 1st ed., pp. 170–2; Toronto and R.K.P. ed., pp. 446–8). He noted an alternative possible explanation in terms of the survival of the fittest, but although elsewhere he had expressed a favourable reaction to the Darwinian theory as an interesting, possibly true hypothesis, his general underestimation of the value of the hypothetical method seems to have influenced him in favour of the alternative account.

Mill's account of the argument from design, contrary to his expressed claim, is not of it as an argument resting on the use of the method of difference. It does not admit of restatement as such, since this method requires that both the antecedent and consequent be observed. In the case of the eye, it is only the consequent that is observed; the antecedent is inferred. Further, even if this argument could be restated as one in terms of the method of agreement, it would then be little stronger than when construed as an argument by analogy, for as Mill so often acknowledged, the method of agreement does not give proof because of the phenomenon of plurality of causes. As an argument by analogy, it is exposed to the fact of evil. Mill's restatement of the argument is exposed to the different objection that where we find *apparent* evidence of intelligent design, we often find no evidence of intelligent planning, but simply a chance concomitance of many causes. The stone which, as a result of the action of the waves, has been made into an object of beauty, is a product of many causes. So too with stalactites and stalagmites. The spider's web may also look as if it is a product of an intelligent mind; so too the carefully constructed bird's nest. We know that they are not such, that neither the spider nor the bird is an intelligent designer. Unless we reject the available explanations in terms of natural causes, there is no need to postulate a supernatural cause; and the structure of the eye, which so impressed Mill, provides no ground for believing in a single, intelligent, planning cause. It might be replied to the above examples that these are precisely the kinds of phenomena from which the theist is arguing. This cannot be so, for with them there is a natural causal explanation, and hence, if anything, they are counter-cases to the thesis that all apparent products of intelligence are found on examination to be such. It is surprising, in view of his argument concerning miracles, that Mill entertained such a supernatural hypothesis when alternative explanations in terms of natural phenomena are available. Mill thought that the argument from design established a probability in favour of the existence of a God who is a planner and a designer but not a creator. He brings about changes in the world but does not create it.

The Attributes of God

Power

In *Nature*, Mill conceded that a Manichaean type of theory was compatible with the facts. In *Theism* he strongly favoured a monotheism with a suggestion concerning the intractability of matter (i.e. a permanent possibility of sensation, according to Mill). The argument for a single God appears to be based on the unity of the plan – this is not fully argued – and the fact that there is no reason for attributing intelligence to the so-called obstacles to God. In *Nature*, Mill had observed: 'The only admissible theory of Creation is that the Principle of Good *cannot* at once and altogether subdue the powers of evil, either physical or moral. . . . Of all the religious explanations of the order of nature, this alone is neither contradictory to itself, nor to the facts for which it attempts to account' (ibid., 1st ed., pp. 38–9; Toronto and R.K.P. ed., pp. 389–90). In *Theism* he rejected Manichaeism, arguing: 'There is no ground in Natural Theology for attributing intelligence or personality to the obstacles which partially thwart what seem the purposes of the Creator. The limitation of his power more probably results either from the qualities of the material . . . or else the Creator did not know how to do it' (ibid., 1st ed., p. 186; Toronto and R.K.P. ed., p. 455). Mill in fact had to choose between claiming that God was all-powerful and morally imperfect, or finite. He chose the latter course, offering as evidence of God's finitude that he used contrivance to achieve his ends, and that he would not have done so had he been able to realise his ends directly. Obviously the use of means to achieve ends is not adequate evidence that the ends cannot be achieved directly. Similarly, if one looks at the world, in particular at the fact of carnivorism, that some must painfully kill and eat others, Mill's suggestion that the evil features of the world lack the character of intelligent planning to be found in the good features rings of special pleading. *Omniscience* is rightly construed as relating to power and as being an essential condition for omnipotence. Mill was agnostic concerning God's claim to omniscience, inclining if anything towards denying it.

Goodness

Mill argued that God can reasonably be thought to be concerned with human happiness, and hence to be benevolent, even though he does not do all he could here. The crux of his argument is that normal processes usually give pleasure rather than pain; that where pain occurs, it is either unintended or a condition for pleasure, or perhaps due to a limitation in God's power. This argument has more than an air of special pleading for a predetermined conclusion, and shows a total disregard for Mill's earlier assessment of the extent and enormity of evil. There is no serious attempt to assess the evidence, yet even with natural processes there is much evidence against the goodness of the planner. Consider our exposure to pain and suffering, and the inefficiency of pain as a warning system. Consider also carnivorism, the pain and evils involved in other natural phenomena, child-bearing, ageing and death. Mill was nearer the truth when in *Nature* he had argued: 'If we are not obliged to believe the animal creation to be the work of a demon, it is because we need not suppose it to have been made by a Being of

170

infinite power. But if imitation of the Creator's will as revealed in nature, were applied as a rule of action in this case, the most atrocious enormities of the worst men would be more than justified by the apparent intention of Providence that throughout all animated nature the strong should prey on the weak' (ibid., 1st ed., pp. 58–9; Toronto and R.K.P. ed., p. 399). Obviously, Mill ought to have adopted a completely agnostic position concerning the attributes of his god. He offered no worthwhile reasons for believing him, it or they to be finite rather than infinite, lazily malevolent rather than half-heartedly benevolent, a personal or non-personal God or gods. This being so, and on the basis of his attack on Mansel, Mill had no adequate grounds for referring to him as God, nor for regarding him as a proper object of worship.

Mill's Critique of Mansel's Account of Our Knowledge of God

As against Mansel, who in *The Limits of Religious Thought* had argued for the unknowability of the attributes of God, that we may attribute goodness, etc., to God but not in any knowable sense, Mill in chap. 7 of *Hamilton* stressed the necessity of a knowledge of God's attributes, especially his goodness, in the ordinary sense of goodness, if he is to be a proper object of religious adoration, awe and worship. Mill's ill-tempered rejection of Mansel's contentions are an aspect of the problem in theistic philosophy concerning what is being asserted when attributes are ascribed to God. Mansel's account is exposed to difficulties, but so too are most other accounts, for they involve to a greater or less degree elements of the agnosticism which renders Mansel's account so unsatisfactory. Thus the account offered in part in traditional theology in terms of the doctrine of analogy, in claiming that pure perfections (power, knowledge, goodness, life) hold of God in a distinct but not equivocal sense to that in which they hold of men, involves, as F. C. Copleston acknowledges, a real element of agnosticism concerning the attributes of God (see *Aquinas*, pp. 134–7).

Immortality

Mill distinguished those arguments concerning immortality which are independent of a theory about God's existence from those which are dependent on that theory. Mill in his discussion of the former is confused, sometimes writing as if matter had a real existence independent of minds, at other times remembering and applying his phenomenalist conclusions. As a phenomenalist Mill was committed to a denial of the existence of matter as a substance distinct from actual and possible sensations; yet he argued: 'Those, therefore, who would deduce the immortality of the soul from its own nature have first to prove that the attributes in question are not attributes of the body but of a separate substance' (*Three Essays*, 1st ed., p. 197; Toronto and R.K.P. ed., p. 460). Mill then, quite inappropriately for a phenomenalist, went on to discuss the dependence of mental phenomena on the condition of the brain, when in fact for him it was the dependence (invariable sequence) of one set of mental phenomena on another. That this was not simply a verbal slip is suggested by the statement that 'the relation of thought to a material brain is no metaphysical necessity; but simply a constant co-existence within the limits of observation' (ibid., 1st ed., p. 199; Toronto and R.K.P. ed., p. 461). At this point he related his phenomenalism to the issue, noting that mind is the only reality of which there is any evidence, and that it may well be 'perishable'. (In the discussion in *Hamilton*, it is only sensations, or possibilities of them, which are imperishable.) Mill then considered various of the arguments that have been offered, noting their obvious inadequacies, and concluded that there is no assurance of immortality from religion. However, in a curious discussion, he allowed the hope of immortality to be reasonable, and even that it may be comforting. This is in sharp contrast with the scientific approach to the arguments for God's existence, and more especially with his treatment of the argument from design.

Concluding Note: Mill's Continuing Relevance and Importance

The foregoing discussion would suggest that Mill's contributions to logic will in the future be of much greater interest to the historian of logic than to practising logicians. His contributions to ethics seem likely to remain of importance as long as utilitarianism is taken seriously as an ethical theory; and that is as long as ethics is taken seriously. In political philosophy the success of some of his writings has made some of them no longer of contemporary importance; none the less, they could again come to be of great importance. Others, most notably the essay *On Liberty*, are likely to become increasingly relevant and important; the considerations in favour of liberty to which Mill pointed, are considerations it is vital that mankind never lose sight of. Mill's presentation of the phenomenalist thesis is even now only of historical interest, and of no continuing importance. His contributions in the area of philosophy of religion, apart from the argument in *Theism*, are of routine interest. *Theism* is likely to continue to be of interest as a museum piece, as containing an argument for a finite God by a great philosopher.

Bibliography

The most complete bibliography of Mill's very extensive writings is that of N. MacMinn, J. R. Hainds and J. McN. McCrimmon, *Bibliography of the Published Writings of John Stuart Mill* (Evanston, Ill., North-western University Press, 1945). This bibliography is based on one kept by Mill himself, and it lists even very minor contributions published during Mill's lifetime. The *Autobiography*, *Three Essays on Religion* and *Chapters on Socialism* were published posthumously.

Short List of the Major Writings of J. S. Mill

A System of Logic (1843; 8th ed., 1872).
Essays on Some Unsettled Questions of Political Economy (1844).
Principles of Political Economy (1848; 7th ed., 1871).
On Liberty (1859).
Dissertations and Discussions (2 vols, 1859; 3 vols, 1867; 4 vols, 1875).
Considerations on Representative Government (1861).
Utilitarianism (1863); originally published in *Fraser's Magazine* (Oct–Dec 1861).
An Examination of Sir William Hamilton's Philosophy (1865; 4th ed., 1872).
Auguste Comte and Positivism (1865); originally published in *Westminster Review* (Apr and July 1865).
Inaugural Address at the University of St Andrews (1867).
The Subjection of Women (1869).
Autobiography, ed. Helen Taylor (1873). See also *The Early Draft of John Stuart Mill's Autobiography*, ed.

J. Stillinger (Urbana, University of Illinois Press, 1961).

Three Essays on Religion (1874).

Chapters on Socialism, reprinted from the *Fortnightly Review* (1879).

Mill also edited James Mill's *Analysis of the Phenomena of the Human Mind* (1869).

Current Editions of Mill's Works

The most important edition today is that which Toronto University Press is preparing, namely, the *Collected Works of John Stuart Mill* (variations in the various editions being noted and published); published in U.K. by Routledge & Kegan Paul. Published to date are:

vols II and III	*Principles of Political Economy*
vols IV and V	*Essays on Economics and Society, 1824–1879*
vol X	*Essays on Ethics, Religion and Society*
vols XII and XIII	*The Earlier Letters, 1812–1848*

Due to be published soon are two volumes of *The System of Logic* and *The Later Letters.* Also in preparation are *The Examination of Sir William Hamilton's Philosophy, Essays on Politics and Society* and the *Autobiography.*

The following are currently available, many in several editions: *System of Logic, Liberty, Utilitarianism, Auguste Comte and Positivism, The Subjection of Women, Autobiography, Theism.* In addition many of the essays included in *Dissertations and Discussions* have recently been once again reprinted. Two of the more useful collections here are *Essays on Politics and Culture,* ed. G. Himmelfarb (New York, Doubleday Anchor, 1963) and *Mill's Ethical Writings,* ed. J. B. Schneewind (London, Collier–Macmillan, 1965).

Mill's Memorandum of the Improvements in the Administration of India During the Last Thirty Years, and the Petition of the East-India Company to Parliament has been reprinted by Gregg International, Farnborough, England, 1968.

Bibliography of Works about Mill

There is today a vast literature in many languages relating to Mill, his life and philosophy. The Toronto University Press *The Mill News Letter* (editor John M. Robson), itself a journal of considerable importance to Mill scholars, contains an excellent comprehensive bibliography of writings concerning and relevant to Mill. The bibliography given below should be supplemented by reference to it.

General Works

Anschutz, R. P., *The Philosophy of J. S. Mill* (Oxford, Clarendon Press, 1953). Chiefly orientated to logical issues but with chapters on ethics and political theory. Carefully argued and good.

Britton, K., *John Stuart Mill* (London, Penguin Books, 1953; reprinted by Dover Publications, New York, 1969). A useful general work, covering the major aspects of Mill's philosophy.

Halévy, É., *The Growth of Philosophical Radicalism* (London, Faber & Faber, 1952). A classic.

Robson, J. M., *The Improvement of Mankind* (Toronto, 1968). A scholarly and able work, which, although described as 'The Social and Political Thought of John Stuart Mill', has more general relevance.

Ryan, A., *The Philosophy of John Stuart Mill* (London, Macmillan, 1970). Develops an interesting interpretation of Mill.

Schneewind, J. B. (ed.), *Mill* (New York, Doubleday Anchor, 1968; London, Macmillan, 1969). An excellent collection of first-rate articles covering the major areas of Mill's philosophy.

Stephen, L., *The English Utilitarians*, esp. vol. III (London, Duckworth, 1900). An important, standard reference.

Biographical Works

Bain, A., *John Stuart Mill: A Criticism* (London, Longmans, Green, 1882). Compact, informative account of Mill's life with interesting philosophical asides.

Borchard, Ruth, *John Stuart Mill: The Man* (London, Watts, 1957). Vividly written, plausible account of Mill's life and interpretation of Mill's personality and character.

Hayek, F. A. von, *John Stuart Mill and Harriet Taylor: Their Friendship and Subsequent Marriage* (London, Routledge & Kegan Paul, 1951). Mainly letters.

Packe, M. St J., *The Life of John Stuart Mill* (London, Secker & Warburg, 1954). The authoritative biography; thorough, scholarly, often perceptive, and interestingly written.

Pappe, H. O., *J. S. Mill and the Harriet Taylor Myth* (Melbourne University Press, 1960). Conclusions a little more plausible than the arguments.

Russell, Bertrand, 'John Stuart Mill', in *Portraits from Memory* (London, Allen & Unwin, 1951). Reprinted in *Mill* (ed. Schneewind) above.

Logic

Eaton, R. M., *General Logic* (New York, Charles Scribner's & Co., 1931). Pt II, chaps II, III, VI, VII; pt IV, chap. II.

Hart, H. L. A., and Honoré, A. M., *Causation in the Law* (Oxford, Clarendon Press, 1959), esp. chap. 1.

Jackson, R., *An Examination of the Deductive Logic of John Stuart Mill* (Oxford University Press, 1941). An able though often obscure work.

Jevons, W. S., *The Principles of Science* (London, Macmillan, 1887).

Joseph, H. W. B., *An Introduction to Logic*, 2nd ed. (Oxford, Clarendon Press, 1916) esp. chaps VI, XIV, XIX, XX.

Mabbott, J. D., 'Two Notes on Syllogism', *Mind*, XLVIII (1939).

Ryle, C., 'The Theory of Meaning', in *British Philosophy in Mid-Century*, ed. C. A. Mace (London, Allen & Unwin, 1957).

Strawson, P. F., *Introduction to Logical Theory* (London, Methuen, 1952), esp. chap. 2, pt II, chap. 9, pt II.

Toulmin, S., *The Philosophy of Science* (London, Hutchinson, 1953).

Ethics

Atkinson, R. F., 'J. S. Mill's Proof of the Principle of Utility', *Philosophy*, XXXII (1957).

Bradley, F. H., *Ethical Studies* (Oxford, Clarendon Press, 1876), esp. Essay 3.

Brandt, R. B., *Ethical Theory* (Englewood Cliffs, N.J., Prentice–Hall, 1959), esp. chaps. 15, 16, 19.

Britton, K., 'Utilitarianism: The Appeal to a First Principle', *Proceedings of the Aristotelian Society*, LX (1959–60).

Hall, E., 'The "Proof" of Utility in Bentham and Mill', *Ethics*, LX (1949).

Kleinig, J., 'The Fourth Chapter of Mill's Utilitarianism', *Australasian Journal of Philosophy*, XLVIII (1970).

Mabbott, J. D., 'Interpretations of Mill's "Utilitarianism"', *Philosophical Quarterly*, VI (1956).

Mandelbaum, M., 'On Interpreting Mill's Utilitarianism', *Journal of the History of Ideas*, VI (1968).

Moore, G. E., *Principia Ethica* (Cambridge University Press, 1903), esp. chap. III.

——, *Ethics* (London, Hutchinson, 1912; paperback ed., Oxford University Press, 1966).

Plamenatz, J., *The English Utilitarians* (Oxford, Blackwell, 1949).

Urmson, J. O., 'The Interpretation of the Moral Philosophy of J. S. Mill', *Philosophical Quarterly*, III (1953).

Collections

Contemporary Utilitarianism, ed. M. D. Bayles (New York, Doubleday Anchor, 1968) is a useful collection of articles relevant to Mill's utilitarian ethics. Other such similarly relevant collections are in preparation with various other publishers, including *Studies in Utilitarianism*, ed. T. K. Hearn, Jr (New York, Appleton–Century–Crofts); *Mill's Utilitarianism*, in Bobbs–Merrill Text and Commentary Series (Indianapolis), ed. S. Gorovitz; and *Mill's Utilitarianism: Critical Studies*, ed. J. Smith and E. Sosa (Belmont, Calif., Wadsworth).

Political Philosophy

Berlin, I., *Four Essays on Liberty* (Oxford University Press, 1969). Includes the celebrated 'Two Concepts of Liberty' and the less well-known, brilliant essay 'John Stuart Mill and the Ends of Life'.

Cowling, M., *Mill and Liberalism* (Cambridge University Press, 1963). A controversial book which represents Mill as an authoritarian.

Green, T. H., *Lectures on the Principles of Political Obligation*, 1st ed. (1890–1900); with introduction by Lord Lindsay (London, Longmans, Green, 1941).

Hobhouse, L. T., *Liberalism* (London, Williams & Norgate, 1911).

Humboldt, W. von, *The Limits of State Action* (1854: *The Sphere and Duties of Government*, trans. J. Couthard), ed. and rev. J. W. Burrow (Cambridge University Press, 1969).

Rees, J. C., *Mill and his Early Critics* (Leicester University College, 1956).

Ritchie, D. G., *Natural Rights* (London, Allen & Unwin, 1894), esp. chaps 7–10.

Schumpeter, J. A., *Capitalism, Socialism and Democracy* (London, Allen & Unwin, 1950), esp. chap. 21.

Stephen, James Fitzjames, *Liberty, Equality, Fraternity* (London, Smith, Elder, 1873; Cambridge University Press, 1967). A great work. The discussion of liberty is more perceptive and relevant than those concerning equality and fraternity.

Tawney, R. H., *Equality* (London, Allen & Unwin, 1931; 4th ed., 1952).

Ten, C. L., 'Mill on Self-Regarding Actions', *Philosophy*, XLIII (1968). Vol. XLIII, no. 1 of *Philosophy* is a J. S. Mill number, and contains other useful articles relating to Mill's political theory and ethics.

West, E. G., 'Liberty and Education: John Stuart Mill's Dilemma', *Philosophy*, XL (1965).

Collection

P. Radcliff (ed.), *Limits of Liberty* (Belmont, Calif., Wadsworth, 1966). Contains articles and extracts. A useful but not eminently satisfactory collection.

Metaphysics

Ayer, A. J., *Foundations of Empirical Knowledge* (London, Macmillan, 1947).

Berlin, I., 'Empirical Propositions and Hypothetical Statements', *Mind*, LIX (1950).

Day, J. P., 'Mill on Matter', *Philosophy*, XXXVIII (1963). Also in *Mill*, ed. Schneewind, above.

Price, H. H., *Perception* (London, Methuen, 1932).

Strawson, P. F., *Individuals* (London, Methuen, 1959).

Collection

R. J. Hirst (ed.), *Perception and the External World* (London, Collier–Macmillan, 1965). A useful collection of relevant writings.

Holland, R. F., 'The Miraculous', *American Philosophical Quarterly*, II (1965).

Hume, D., *An Enquiry Concerning the Human Understanding*, section 10, pt 1.

Kant, I., *Critique of Pure Reason*, Second Division, 'Transcendental Dialectic', bk 2, chap. 3.

Nowell-Smith, P. H., 'Miracles'; in *New Essays in Philosophical Theology*, ed. A. Flew and A. MacIntyre (London, Student Christian Movement, 1955).

Collections

J. Hick (ed.), *The Existence of God* (London, Collier–Macmillan, 1964). Contains writings relevant to topics to which Mill addressed himself in *Three Essays on Religion. New Essays in Philosophical Theology* still of use, although dating fast.

Index

Socrates, 66, 69
Sosa, E., 180
Spencer, Herbert, 15, 112, 128
Spinoza, B. de, 143
Stephen, J. Fitzjames, 108, 114, 123, 136, 181
Stephen, L., 178
Sterling, J., 10, 13
Stewart, Dugald, 20, 32
Stillinger, J., 176
Strawson, P. F., 49, 50, 179, 181
Stuart, Sir John, 9
Syllogism, 22-8
Synthetic *a priori*, 27, 29, 32, 55, 84

Tawney, R. H., 139, 181
Taylor, Harriet (*née* Hardy), Mrs, 7, 11-14, 111, 137
Taylor, Helen, 14-15, 161, 175
Taylor, Henry, 10
Taylor, John (husband of Harriet), 11-12
Ten, C. L., 181

Tennyson, Alfred (later Lord), 13
Thirwall, C., 10
Thornton, W., 15, 139
Tocqueville, A. de, 14, 99, 135
Toulmin, S., 48, 179
Townshend, Professor, 9

Uniformity of nature, 49-55
Urmson, J. O., 79, 179
Utilitarianism, 56-95
   act, 75-8
   rule, 79-84
Utility, Principle of, 59

Villiers, C. and H., 10

West, E. G., 181
Westminster Review, 10
Whately, R., 16, 22
Whewell, W., 16, 32, 35, 43, 75
Wilberforce, S., 10
Wittgenstein, L., 20
Women, equality of, 135-7
Wordsworth, W., 11

186